COLOSSIANS

COLOSSIANS

COLOSSIANS
Oneness With Christ

by

W. R. NICHOLSON

Edited by

JAMES M. GRAY
Late President, Moody Bible Institute

KREGEL PUBLICATIONS
Grand Rapids, Michigan 49501

This edition published by Kregel Publications, a division of Kregel, Inc., under special arrangements with Moody Press, successors to the Bible Institute Colportage Association.

First Kregel Publication Edition 1951
Second Printing 1966
Third Printing 1973

Library of Congress Catalog Card Number 73-81742

ISBN 0-8254-3301-0

CONTENTS

INTRODUCTION

I AM about to begin what I anticipate as one of the most delightful, and, in some respects, the most spiritually fruitful tasks of my whole life. It is the editing of the expository lectures on Colossians of my beloved friend and overseer in the Lord, the late Bishop William R. Nicholson, D.D., of Philadelphia—"an eloquent man, and mighty in the Scriptures." The feast of my own soul in the perusal of his manuscript I am impatient to share with as large a constituency of my fellow-believers as I can possibly reach, for such teaching, as to its deep insight into spiritual things, its vigor of appeal, its heavenly unction, its grace of manner and beauty of diction, is not commonly met with in this or any other day. And then the theme! Paul's letter to the Colossians, in which he touches the very high-water mark of divinely-revealed truth, the Person and the Glory of Jesus Christ. Oh, for the Spirit of Christ to rest upon writer and reader as we proceed together in the blessed subject of this study.

But I am reminded that some do not know Bishop Nicholson as I and others knew him, and this introductory word is to tell them something about him.

Of Southern extraction (his father was a county judge in Mississippi before the war), he graduated from La Grange College, Alabama, and was ordained as presbyter (he never permitted himself to be called "priest") in the Protestant Episcopal Church, in 1847, by Bishop Polk, afterwards of military fame under the Confederacy. His charges in that denomination were of the highest order almost from the very beginning—Grace, New Orleans; St. John's, Cincinnati; St. Paul's, Boston, and Trinity, Newark. The rectorship of the last-named parish he resigned on conscientious grounds, to throw in his lot with the newly organized Reformed Episcopal denomination, then (1873) coming into life under the leadership of Bishop George David Cummins, of Kentucky. Here he was chosen rector of St. Paul's, Philadelphia, and two years later consecrated Bishop of the Synod of New York and Philadelphia. At the foundation of the Reformed Episcopal Theological Seminary subsequently, he was appointed Dean of the Faculty, and Professor of Exegesis and Pastoral Theology, which multitudinous responsibilities he continued to perform practically until the time of his death, full of years and of honors, on June 7, 1901.

Bishop Cheney, in referring to his earliest impressions of him, speaks especially of his *power*. "Possibly his grand physical frame, towering stature, and almost majestic presence contributed to this result. But when one came to hear him in public address, there was a massive force in his marshalling of his arguments, and sledge-hammer weight in his reasoning, which made the listener, whether he agreed or disagreed with his conclusions, feel that whatever else Bishop Nicholson was, he was an intellectual athlete, a spiritually strong man."

I quote, somewhat freely, the language of his successor as Dean of the Seminary, Rev. J. Howard Smith, D.D.: "It is not enough to say he was eminently endowed in the general, undiscriminated sense of the words. I think it not too much to say his mind was singularly analytical and logical. He never wrote in a haze. No trace of indeterminateness can be found in any of his discussions on any subject. His insight pierced through all the intricacies of the matter in hand. His exegesis was always minute. Though I could not always appropriate its conclusions, I could not fail to admire its keen glance into every relation of his text or subject and its practical sequences in exposition."

"But the Bishop was not only the acute analyst and logician. He was endowed with vivid powers of imagination. He had not the soaring fancy of a Chalmers or of a Beecher. His flights were more grave, and they clung more closely to the realities of conviction and the simple unfoldings of truth. But when he had a great subject as the solid ground from which to mount, he could soar and bear his audience with him in his flights. Dr. Sparrow, a profound thinker, a keen logician, of deep emotional nature, but emotion under educated control, after listening to one of Dr. Nicholson's great sermons in the time of his best development of power, paused repeatedly on the street to give excited expression to astonishment and admiration. I well remember an outcrying burst of excitement from a man in the midst of one of Bishop Nicholson's great lectures, an outburst in which, I suspect, the whole audience sympathized. In some of his greatest efforts, when in the prime of early manhood, the absorption of mind, the spiritual fervor that held the audience in spellbound interest, regardless of the lapse of time, rose to an intensity holding captive his entire conscious life. I remember one occasion when, at the close of a discourse of overwhelming power, I began to speak to him on the subject. It was only after some moments that the Bishop could descend to my level enough to understand my words. Those who have heard him on such occasions can never forget the scenes and the impressions."

Another authority, competent to speak, Bishop Hoffman, D.D., declares that Bishop Nicholson saw God's truth not as other men see it, but by direct vision. "He learned it not from others, nor from books, though he was a most careful student of other men's thoughts. The unseen things of God were revealed to his own intuitions through painstaking waiting before God and sweet communion with his Lord and Saviour. Thus, under the intense light of spirituality, as few, he saw the inner truth and hidden glories of the Holy Scriptures. To his view the Bible was from beginning to end luminous with the splendors of Christ. Then what a marvelous gift was his to reveal to others the unsearchable riches of Christ. His vision of the truth materialized. His dreams, like Bunyan's, were capable of interpretation in the vivid language of human speech, appealing to man's deepest consciousness of need. What an uplift there was in his matchless expositions of the Word! How by his clear analysis, spiritual insight and sublime logic, he inspired faith to a wider sweep of privilege and blessing! How, as he unveiled the new beauties and immeasurable wealth of Christ, he made contagious his own personal joy and ecstasy!"

The same writer bears testimony to how his own conceptions of Christ were "broadened and clarified" by listening to these very lectures on Colossians, with which it will soon be our pleasure to become acquainted in another form. "As long as memory holds the tablet that records past events," he exclaims, "will I recall that Tuesday afternoon when Bishop Nicholson unfolded the glorious significance of Colossians i. 13-20. My heart has ever since beaten with a new and deeper joy because of the wider view of blessedness and glory in Christ I had then given me. He gave me food for thought that afternoon upon which my heart has since been nourished."

But enough. We have now been introduced to the man, our next contribution will introduce us to his work.

James. M. Gray.

1

THE PLACE AND THE PEOPLE

COLOSSÆ was situated in the Roman province of Asia, of which the chief city was Ephesus, on the Agean Sea. At the mouth of the Mæander, about seventy-five miles south of Ephesus, was the city of Miletus, where the elders of the Church of Ephesus met the Apostle Paul (Acts xx). We go up the Mæander, in a northeasterly direction, to its junction with the Lycus, then up the Lycus, yet more easterly, to the cities of Laodicea and Hierapolis, about one hundred and twenty-five miles from the mouth of the Mæander; then up the Lycus ten or twelve miles further to Colossæ. Thus the three cities, Laodicea, Hierapolis and Colossæ, lay very near to each other, and whatever were the general influences—whether commercial, political or philosophical—pervading any one of the cities, would belong more or less to the other two.

Laodicea was famous for its wealth, and also for its philosophers, sophists and rhetoricians. Hierapolis was distinguished as the birthplace of Epictetus, the greatest of heathen moralists, and a contemporary of the great Apostle. Phrygia, the "region" containing Colossæ, had been long famous as the adopted home of Oriental mysticism. Under such influences false doctrine might be expected to spring up in the churches of those cities, and at once we are prepared for the general character of this letter to the Colossians.

It is almost certain that the church at Colossæ was not planted by Paul himself, and that he had never visited that city when he wrote the epistle. The Acts do not require us to believe that he had. The epistle speaks of his knowing the Colossian Christians by report (i. 4, 9). He makes no mention of any personal incident as having occurred during a sojourn among them; and yet it was his ordinary practice to refer to such incidents in his epistles written to particular churches among whom he had labored. And, finally, Col. ii. 1, proves that the Colossians had never seen his face in the flesh.

On the other hand, the presumption is a fair one, from chapters i 4-8, and iv. 12, 13, that Epaphras was the founder of this church, as

well as those in Laodicea and Hierapolis.
And yet Colossæ was no doubt one of the
fruits of Paul's labors after all, as we may
gather from the story of his work in Ephesus
near by, recorded in Acts xix. 10, 26, for example. The intercourse between Ephesus
and the surrounding country was close and
frequent, and Epaphras and Philemon, from
Colossæ, and Nymphas, from Laodicea, may
be supposed to have come under the apostle's preaching.

It may certainly be concluded that he
wrote this epistle near the close of his first
Roman captivity (Acts xxviii.), at about the
year 62 or 63. From three to six years had
passed, then, since he had left Ephesus, and
during that interval the Church had been established in the three cities, and the development of false doctrine reported by Epaphras
had occurred. This false doctrine was a
mixture of Judaism (ii. 16) and Oriental
mystic speculation (ii. 18).

That there were Jews in large numbers in
that region of the country is certain, and that
there was a Jewish sect precisely answering to
the false doctrine condemned in this epistle is
certain. The sect was known as the Essenes,
who, unlike the Pharisees and Sadducees, do
not appear in the Gospel narratives, because

their principles withdrew them from the daily life of the Jewish people and immured them in convents. They were essentially a Gnostic sect, and Gnosticism, under whatever variety, was characterized by three all-pervading features: (1) An exclusive spirit. The word means one who claims pre-eminent knowledge, an aristocrat in wisdom, an intellectual caste with, in this case, a process and oaths of initiation. (2) Speculative tenets on creation, evil, emanations, angels. Creation was not by the Supreme God, since He could have nothing to do with matter which is inherently evil, but by one or more of the angelic emanations from Him. Those emanations or angels are to be worshipped. (3) Ethical practice. Either a rigid asceticism, because of matter being the abode of evil, or unrestrained licentiousness, on the principle of not condescending to care at all about a thing so inherently evil as is matter.

Now, in the Epistle to the Colossians, Paul assails the exclusive spirit of intellectual caste (i. 28). As in other epistles, he insists upon the free offer of the Gospel to all men, but now from a different point of view. Here it is as opposing *intellectual* exclusiveness; not, as in Galatians, *national* exclusiveness. Perfection was a great Gnostic word, and that word the apostle here appropriates to the position in Christ of every believer. He also attacks the speculative tenets of angelology and the idolatrous practice of angelolatry (i. 15-19; ii. 18), opposing to them both the true ideas of Christ in His Person and His mediation. And he utters his condemnation of a very peculiar ethical practice (Col. ii. 16, 23), protesting not alone against "holy days, new moons, and Sabbaths" (strictly Jewish observances), but against the asceticism with regard to "drinks," and the "neglecting of the body" (which was wholly of Gnostic origin) ; and opposing to both the Jewish and the Gnostic practices the believer's life in Christ.

It has been well said that the Colossian heresy was no vulgar falsehood. At the bottom of it there was an earnest, yearning, unsatisfied desire of the soul; a sense of need unrequited; an aching void the world had never filled. In its doctrine of the mediation of angels and the consequent removal of God from contact with the inherent evil of matter, it claimed to honor the supreme majesty of the Deity, and at the same time to show forth its own humility, as shrinking amid the evils of human nature, from any direct converse with God; while yet in its asceticism it honored itself and ministered to the pride and vanity of

self-righteousness. It was human nature as
essentially displayed everywhere and in all
ages; the circumstances and the particular
tenets ever changing, but the affectation of humility and the proud, self-righteous spirit ever
remaining the same. And thus it is that the
Colossian heresy was an anticipation of the
errors of today, and that the apostles' confutation of it supplies the needed instruction for
ourselves.

[Every one at all familiar with the teachings of Christian Science, so-called, and the
principles of that form of Buddhism known as
Theosophy, will at once appreciate the force of
this remark.—ED.]

The Essene, upon becoming a Christian,
would naturally strive to combine his distinctive principles more or less with the Gospel.
The effect would be to modify and pervert the
Gospel, first with regard to the Person of
Christ, since by his theory of infinitely removing the Deity from any connection with matter
he was tempted to lower Him, as occupying
the office of Mediator, to a mere angelic emanation from the Deity; and, secondly, with regard
to Christ's redemption, since by his theory of
the efficacy of ascetic observances he was
tempted to eviscerate and impoverish the whole
idea of salvation through the merits of the

Saviour's work, finished once for all. In both these regards the Epistle to the Colossians is a storehouse of Christly truth and of the principles of evangelical holiness.

2

THE SALUTATION

SAINTSHIP AND SANCTIFICATION--RELATION OF
GRACE AND PEACE.   (Chapter i. 1, 2.)

"Paul, an apostle of Christ Jesus, by the will of
God, and Timothy, the brother, to the saints at Colossæ, and faithful brethren in Christ. Grace unto you,
and peace from God our Father."

THE reader will notice the changes in the
text which approximate those of the margin of the Revised Version.

1. *Observe Paul's designation of himself:*
"An apostle of Jesus Christ by the will of
God." "An apostle," Paul's differences in designating himself are remarkable. In I. and
II. Thessalonians, simply "Paul." In Titus,
"servant of God and apostle of Christ Jesus."
In II. Corinthians, Ephesians, Colossians, II.
Timothy, "apostle of Christ Jesus by the will
of God." In Galatians, "an apostle, not from
men, neither by man, but by Jesus Christ and
God the Father." Certainly these variations
were not accidental. As to the Colossians, we
can see, in the fact of the epistle being written

to confute serious error, a reason for his designating himself an apostle. "Apostle of Christ Jesus." Both as having been sent by Christ, and as being the servant of Christ in the work of his apostolate. "By the will of God." Not by personal merit, but by God's sovereign good pleasure. His thankful remembrance of God's grace, and his feeling of obedience to His will. Not alone the apostolate, but the entire Christian ministry, is by the will of God. (Eph. iv. 11.)

2. *Observe his designation of Timothy.* "And Timothy the brother." This was not because of Timothy bearing any part in the composition of the epistle, since after the introduction the plural is dropped, and Paul speaks in his own person alone, but because of the affection of the apostle. The sentence, "Paul, an apostle of Christ Jesus, and Timothy the brother," seems to exclude Timothy from being an apostle. See also II. Corinthians i. 1. And when Paul links Timothy's name with his own under the same designation, he drops the title of apostle, as in Philippians i. 1, "Paul and Timothy, servants of Jesus Christ." Yet the apostolate was not confined to the Twelve and Paul. Barnabas, Acts xiv. 4, 14. James, the Lord's brother, I. Corinthians xv. 5, 7, Galatians i. 19. What, then, was the ground of the

distinction? The having seen Christ seems to
have been one of the necessary conditions of
the apostolic office, I. Corinthians ix. 1, 2, Acts
i. 8; to say nothing of the distinct commission
from Him.

But this designation of Timothy is very
beautiful in itself. Timothy, *the brother,* not
"our" brother. Although so eminent a minister of Christ, yet he is not referred to in any
hierarchical sense, but just as a fellow Christian, a fellow believer, Paul's own kindred in
Christ.

3. *Observe his designation of Christians.*
"The Saints." This is one of the most frequent designations of Christ's people. And
mark, it is given to every believer in Christ,
whether or not pre-eminent for practical holiness. The apostle speaks of "the collection for
the saints"; that is, for all poor Christians
(I. Corinthians xvi. 1). Again, "Salute every
saint in Christ Jesus;" that is, every Christian
at Philippi (Philippians iv. 21). The Gospel
significance of this name is shown by Hebrews
x. 10, "We are sanctified (made saints)
through the offering of the body of Christ once
for all." If we are under the value of the
blood of Christ, thereby we are sanctified, made
saints, made holy, set apart to God as His own
treasure, His jewels. But he that believeth on

Christ is under the value of His blood. Every believer is a saint. And out of this most perfect judicial sanctification, if the truth of it is realized, flows forth, in the strength of the joy of the Lord, all practical sanctification. Oh, that Christians appreciated the inseparable saintship of their position in Christ!

"And faithful brethren in Christ." An additional designation of the same persons. Not only saints, but brethren; members of one family, the family of God. Not merely fellow men, but by a sacred birth, the birth of the Spirit, born into a new brotherhood, a brotherhood in Christ, the brotherhood of redeemed ones. Brethren, in that they are saints. And faithful brethren, in that they were acting in the power of their realized new life in Christ. This word "faithful," while sometimes being used as the equivalent of believing, as in John xx. 27 (the Greek), also means trusty (Luke xii. 42). The character of this epistle, as being directed against certain errors which had begun to appear at Colossæ, requires the latter meaning. The brethren who stood firm in spite of the errors around them.

4. *Observe his designation of the Christian's gifts.* "Grace unto you, and peace, from God our Father."

"Grace." Favor, pure and undeserved. The

good pleasure of God's will (Eph. i. 5). The well-spring of all mercies to sinners. Our salvation, and our continual strengthening, are all "to the praise of the glory of His grace" (Eph. i. 6).

"Peace." The result of our acceptance of the grace. Peace with God, peace in the conscience (Rom. v. 1) ; our enmity to Him subdued, His controversy with us passed. Especially "the peace of God" (Philippians iv. 7), "the peace of Christ" (true reading, Col.iii. 15) ; the peace which the Holy Spirit, as showing the things of Christ" (true reading, Col. iii. 15) ; the peace like a river, which passeth understanding, which "keeps our hearts and minds through Christ Jesus," amid whatever dangers, or trials, or temptations.

Grace and Peace. What blessings are they! The saints at Colossæ needed them for their security against the false teaching beginning to show itself there. And they are the blessings which, for *our* security, we need to have in greater and yet greater abundance, in this day of daring speculation and "liberal" theology.

"From God our Father." This is the only instance in the salutations of Paul's epistles, where the Father's name stands alone, not being associated with that of Christ. Remembering what was said in the preceding chapter concerning the Gnostic heresy, which relegated the Supreme Being to so infinite a remove from any communication with sinful men, and which attempted to supply His place with intermediate angels or emanations, it will seem to us, I think, that the apostle here strikes that heresy in this particular form of salutation. He uses the Father's name alone, that, in its singleness and majesty, the Colossians might be the more emphatically impressed with the loving interest of even the Almighty and Supreme toward sinners. God the Father is gracious, God the Father giveth peace.

A Personal Application.

1. Let us realize the two-fold relationship of a Christian. As toward God, a *saint,* as toward other Christians, a *brother.* These relations are full of blessedness and power. Our daily life should be the practical development of both saintship and brotherhood. It is our responsibility that we be found faithful.

2. At the same time let us understand that grace and peace are the twofold blessedness of those relations. The salutation of the text is a prayer for the bestowal of these blessings, but also it is an apostolic enunciation of the established connection between the relations and the blessings. Because we occupy those relations, it is our privilege and duty to enjoy

these blessings. The Colossian believers were already in possession of grace and peace, else they had not been saints and brethren, and yet Paul prays that they should have a richer possession. Because of what had been given, they might look for yet more to be given. With the grace of God in the soul, and the peace of God ruling in the heart, we are enabled to "walk before the Lord in all well-pleasing."

3

THE THANKSGIVING
ITS OBJECT, NATURE, AND THE REASONS FOR IT

"We give thanks to the God and Father of our
Lord Jesus Christ, praying always for you, having
heard of your faith in Christ Jesus, and of the love
which ye have to all the saints because of the hope
which is laid up for you in the heavens.

"Whereof ye heard before in the Word of the truth
of the Gospel, which is come to you, as also in all the
world it is bringing forth fruit and increasing, as
also among you since the day ye heard and knew
the grace of God in truth; as ye learned from Epaphras, our beloved fellow-servant, who is for us a
faithful minister of Christ, who also declared unto us
your love in the Spirit" (i. 3-8).

1. *Observe that the apostle gave thanks.*
"We give thanks."

HOW important is this express mention
of thanksgiving! The Psalmist is a
great master of thanks; but so also
is our apostle, as his epistles testify. In
this epistle his thanksgivings are like the
refrain of a song. The giving of thanks
is our *answerings* to God. It is the circulation of divine life; from God to us, from
us back to God. Without it there is scarce any
assertion of the real glory of the Gospel. It is

conscious peace, and conscious joy, and conscious victory. Oh, that we appreciated it and were more abundant in the exercise of it! It were a social power to the minister in his shepherding of the flock, and to the private Christian in his various relations.

2. *Observe to whom he gave thanks.* "To the God and Father of our Lord Jesus Christ." Of course he impliedly gave thanks also to the Lord Jesus Christ, and to the Holy Ghost, for They Three are One in nature and purpose. But *distinctively* to God the Father he gave thanks. HIM the Gnostic heresy, as we have seen, pushed far out of all connection with sinful man and his interests. The apostle's thanksgiving is, therefore, an argument of inspired authority against that heresy. God the Father is specially concerned with all that concerns us. The giver of our blessings, He is the object of our thanks and our worship.

Moreover, "the God and Father of the Lord Jesus Christ" is the *Gospel* name of God; for while that name is founded in the very nature of Deity, yet is it the name under which He has revealed Himself to us as the Pardoner of sin and the Saviour of sinners, as having "so loved the world, that He gave His only begotten Son, that whosoever believeth in Him should not perish, but have everlasting life."

It is the completed name of God's self-revelation to us. A fuller and richer name than "the God of Abraham, and of Isaac, and of Jacob" (Ex. iii. 6, 16). For although both are covenant names, yet God's great covenant of grace was neither ratified nor accomplished till the Lord Jesus had shed His blood for sinners, thereby making possible to them the free and boundless grace of the covenant. Here, then, the apostle is giving thanks to God in His character as the Pardoner of sin to every believer in Christ. Nor, since we are sinners, is it possible for us to thank Him acceptably for any of His blessings bestowed upon us, except we do so in the power of those ideas which are suggested by the name, "the God and Father of the Lord Jesus Christ."

3. *Observe for whom he gave thanks.* "For you."

The apostle gave thanks for others, not in this instance for himself. What Gospel love, unselfishness and sympathy this shows, and what a breadth of gratitude toward God! Whoever truly thanks God for himself will also thank Him for others. Our fellow Christian's interest must be ours also.

4. *Observe how* (*or in what connection*) *he gave thanks.* "We give thanks * * * praying always for you."

The apostle gave thanks for the Colossians only in connection with his *praying for* them. Prayer and thanksgiving are inseparable. The sense of dependence which petitions in the one, *rejoices* in the other. There is no true prayer without faith in Christ; but if faith in Him we have, then is prayer answered, and the answer attunes the soul to thanks. No prayer without thanksgiving. On the other hand, the spirit of thanks gives honor to the unstinted bountifulness of our gracious God, and is ever the receptiveness for additional blessings; it is, therefore, the promoter of *largeness* in prayer. No thanksgiving without prayer. Twins of one divine birth. The elements of Christian power in the world.

5. *Observe for what he gave thanks.* "Having heard of your faith in Christ Jesus, and of the love which ye have to all the saints because of the hope which is laid up for you in the heavens."

The words "having heard" are in the aorist tense in the Greek, which expresses the fact that he had heard of their faith and love on some particular occasion, and points to his interview with Epaphras who had come from Colossæ to visit him now in prison at Rome.

(1) He gave thanks for their "faith in Christ Jesus." A faith not only *on* Christ, but

also *in* Him. Which had Christ not alone for
its object, but as well for its sphere; which,
while apprehending Him as dying for their
sins, did so under those Scriptural ideas of
Christ and His work, whereby they were enabled to do justice to that great transaction.
They believed *on* Christ, but they did so *in*
Christ; as *thinking* Christ, and *realizing*
Christ. It was, therefore, a clear faith, and a
strongly operative faith. In thanking God for
their faith in Christ Jesus, then, he was joyously thinking of them as having been *born again,*
and as being *sons of God,* as having been *for-*
given all their sins, and as being *"the right-*
eousness of God in Christ," and as being themselves aware of all this, and enjoying the comfort of their salvation in Him.

(2) He gave thanks for their "love to all the
saints." It was their love to *saints,* to *all*
saints, for which the apostle gave thanks in
their behalf. This is a very specific love. It is
distinguished from love to men as men; it is
love to the brotherhood in Christ (II. Pet. i. 7;
Gal. vi. 10; I. Thess. iii. 12). Such love is the
image of our love to Christ Himself, for, as
loving the saints, we love those who are in
Him, and in whom He is.

The apostle thanked God, then, for the Christian fellowship of the Colossian believers, for

their gentleness and mutual service and faithfulness one toward another.

This love which they had to all the saints
grew out of their hope, their mutual "hope laid
up for them in the heavens." This hope was,
of course, an objective thing, laid up in the
heavens, and yet, inasmuch as he regards it as
operating on and enkindling their love, the objective merges into the subjective. The feeling of hope, as well as the object of hope, exists
in the sentence. Compare I. Thessalonians i. 3.

Therefore (3), he gave thanks not only for
their faith and love, but their enjoyment also
of the grace of hope. There was a reflex action upon them of those heavenly treasures to
which they were entitled in Christ. They *realized* the things hoped for (Tit. ii. 13; Heb. vi.
18). See especially Romans viii. 24, 25, where
the thought plays between the thing and the
feeling. And they realized it as *laid up* for
them; as *secured* for their future actual possession (I. Pet. i. 4, 5). They realized, too,
that a *kingdom* was that which was in rever-
sion for them. The plural "heavens," is suggestive of this, since the phrase "kingdom of
heaven" is always, in the original Greek,
"kingdom of (or in) the heavens"; and the
apostle uses the plural here as seeming to take
for granted that his Colossian readers were

familiar with the force of it. What magnificent treasures! And the believers at Colossæ
thought of them, and felt the reflex action of
the future glory. It was their heavenly-mindedness for which Paul gave thanks to God.
For not only was it an exalted and delicious
feeling, it was also a mighty practical power;
it affected their love to the saints, and kindled
it to a brighter flame. And does not the realization of our interests in heaven always have
this effect? Heirs together of eternal life, and
destined sharers together of the powers and
honors of the kingdom in the heavens, how
shall we not regard each other with an ever-
deepening home affection?

THE MISSION OF EPAPHRAS.

The concluding part of the thanksgiving,
verses 5-8, referring particularly to the service
of Epaphras, first to the Christians at Colossæ
and afterwards to the apostle himself, may be
dismissed with a few words of explanation.

The "whereof" refers to the hope of which
they had heard. "The word of the truth of the
Gospel," means the preaching of that truth
which belongs to the Gospel. "In all the
world," does not mean literally in every place,
and yet it is not, properly speaking, a hyper-
bole. The world was the proper area of the

preached Gospel, and in this sense it was the whole world.

"Bringing forth fruit and increasing," is interesting. The former phrase is in the middle voice, and carries an intensive meaning, an inherent energy of fruit-bearing. It expresses internal fruitfulness, while the latter expresses outward extension. The fruit-bearing of the Gospel, in other words, is not like corn, which having borne fruit, dies, even to its roots, but like a tree, which bears fruit and at the same time continues to grow. The power of the Gospel, the apostle would say, is one and the same everywhere; but those errors of yours, ye Colossians, are indigenous to your own soil, local, and have no fruit-bearing power.

"Heard and knew the grace of God in truth." The grace of God—*the Gospel* (Acts xx. 24; II. Cor. vi. 1; viii. 9). The false gospel at Colossæ was not *grace,* but *ordinances* (ii. 14); not *of God,* but *of the world,* and *of men* (ii. 8, 20, 22). The Colossians had heard this grace of God *in truth,* according as Epaphras had truly proclaimed it; and they had come to know it *in truth*—to know it for just what it is in its power and blessedness.

PRACTICAL LESSONS

We learn from all this (1), that the Gospel is the power of God, as among the Colossians,

so in all the world, fruit-bearing and still grow-
ing (Rom. i. 16, 17; John x. 5).

(2) That we need to hear and know this
Gospel in truth. Here is a responsibility for
both teacher and taught, preacher and hearer.
The simplicity which is in Christ needs to be
safeguarded in either case. How distinctly
stands out Epaphras in contrast with the speculative thinkers of Colossæ. He taught simply
the grace of God.

(3) That the Gospel is meant to be a traveler
"in all the world." Now its power of traveling
is in the fact of its fruitfulness in individual
hearts. Enjoyers of the Gospel are they who
must extend it. Accordingly, how necessary
to be conversant with the hope laid up for us in
the heavens. This hope reacts, and stimulates
and sustains our love. We cannot be selfish,
we cannot become contracted within ourselves,
while our spirits are dilating with appreciations of the joy set before us, the joy and
power of heavenly-mindedness.

4

THE PRAYER

A SINGLE PETITION, BUT A GREAT SCOPE

"For this cause we also, since the day we heard, do not cease praying for you, and beseeching that ye may be filled with the thorough knowledge of His will in all spiritual wisdom and understanding, to walk worthily of the Lord unto all pleasing" (i. 9, 10).

"FOR this cause," means on account of their faith and love spoken of previously. This which follows is the response of Paul's personal feeling to the favorable news he had heard of them, with reference to their faith and love. For this cause he prays for them.

1. *Consider his act of prayer.* He prayed even for those who were saints. We are to be helpers of each other's faith and love; and prayer is one of the strong arms of our power. It might have seemed that, as they were already saints, the apostle should have concentrated his whole interest in prayer upon the unconverted, even as some now say, that all preaching should be addressed to the uncon-

verted. But not so thought the inspired Paul.
There are babes in Christ, and they need to
grow. Even the young men in Christ have yet
to be perfected in all the exercises of practical
consecration. Nay, the very fathers in Christ
have not yet attained to the measure of the
stature of the fulness of Christ. As at every
stage we need to be *taught* more and more, so
we need to be evermore in prayer for each
other. It is the principle as well of the prayer
meeting as of private prayer. But this was a
very special intercession for the saints, especially called forth by what the apostle had
heard of their Christian life and progress. He
could not but respond in prayer because of his
consequent personal sympathy and delight.
Because the very fellowship of Christian hearts
is suggestive of yet further needs and blessings.
Because the salvation already given to the believer is but the earnest to him of the fulness of
the blessing of the Gospel; and is, therefore,
an encouragement to largeness in prayer.

2. *Consider the subject matter of his prayer.*
"That ye may be filled with the thorough
knowledge of His will in all spiritual wisdom
and understanding." This is the one only petition of the whole prayer, all else in the text,
and the words following, being but results of
this petition as answered. How rich in sig-

nificance, then, must be the subject matter of this petition! To be filled with the thorough knowledge of God's will is more than "to know the grace of God in truth" (verse 6). This latter knowledge the Colossians already had. God's *will* here is His revealed will. The knowledge of what He has said in the Bible.

A *thorough* knowledge is a deep, accurate and comprehensive acquaintance with God's expression of Himself in His Word. With Christ in His relations with the Father and His relations with believers. With the Holy Ghost in His relations with Christ and with the believer. With the believer's full standing in grace. With the joys of assurance. With the practical humility of it all, and the holiness to which it leads.

To be *filled* with such thorough knowledge of God's will is to have it pervading our thoughts, and affections, and purposes and plans. It is neither a smattering of the Gospel nor such profound knowledge as is merely intellectual. At the same time the being filled brings enlargement, and so the being filled is an ever continuing process.

Now, this implies the loving, diligent, persevering study of the Word, and thereunto the use of all means in our power. The study of it, not to become learned, but, in the becoming learned, to become filled with the heavenly power of such learning.

We should be filled with it *in all spiritual wisdom and understanding.* *Wisdom* is the knowledge of the best means for attaining to the best ends. But the knowledge of moral and spiritual things is essentially conditioned by a state of sympathy with them. We must love such things in order to know them. So that wisdom, in the spiritual sphere of our being, is very much the same with a true *spiritual taste.* Hence, Psalm cxi. 10; Job xxviii. 28; James iii. 15, 17. To be filled in all spiritual wisdom is to be pervaded by a thorough knowledge of God's will in the clearness and the power of our heart's sympathy with that will. A real relish for it, and, therefore, a clear appreciation of it.

Understanding, as here used, is the correct apprehension of particular things, knowing the bearing of things (Luke ii. 47; Eph. iii. 4; II. Tim. ii. 7). It is an issue of wisdom. To be filled in all spiritual understanding is so to be pervaded by a thorough knowledge of God's will in all wisdom, that we are able to think in accordance with God's will with regard to particular things; as, for instance, whether it be right for a Christian to indulge in certain amusements, or to engage in certain kinds of

business. The spiritual understanding of particular things is the explanation and verifica-
tion of those beautiful words of the Psalmist,
"I will guide thee with Mine eye" (xxxii. 8).

But this wisdom and this understanding are
spiritual, produced and sustained by the Holy
Spirit (I. Cor. ii. 9, 10, 12, 14). The contrasts
to this are expressed in Colossians ii. 8, 18, 23;
II. Corinthians i. 12; I. Corinthians i. 20, ii. 5,
6, 13, iii. 19. So that in studying the Word of
God diligently, we should habitually refer ourselves to the teaching of the Holy Spirit.

Such was the apostle's petition. We see that
the knowledge of God's will is at the foundation of all Christian growth and efficiency.
Acts of worship and of doing good to others
are not enough; we must be also learners of
the Word.

3. *Consider the object of his prayer,* i.e., the
practical result of it as answered. "To walk
worthily of the Lord (or of Christ) unto all
pleasing." (1) To walk. Faith is not a dead
thing, the believer is alive and journeying.
(2) To walk worthily of Christ, suited. fitted
to Him in all His relations with the believer.
The verses to follow tell us particularly about
this walk, but at present it suffices to say that
it should be such living as is answerable to
Christ as our Successful Saviour; as our Vital

Head, with whom we are one, and in whose power of life we actually share; and as our Forerunner into heaven, in whose exaltation we have part even now.   (3) A walk in these regards so faithful and true that it shall be *unto all pleasing.*   With a true Christian, God may be displeased, though He condemn not; and then there is a lack of felt fellowship. Only as walking worthily of *Christ* can we abound in obedience to God, and be as children intimate with their father.   Every Christian's habitual question should be, not, "What must I do to escape censure, or win wages?"   But, "What will please God?"

Let us remember in closing, that a Christian walk of this character is to be secured, not by observing times of prayer simply, nor by the use of ordinances, nor by self-denials, but only by our being kept filled with the thorough knowledge of God's will in all spiritual wisdom and understanding.

5

THE CHRISTIAN'S WALK

ITS PROCESS AND CHARACTER

"Bringing forth fruit in every good work, and increasing by the thorough knowledge of God; strengthened with all strength, according to the power of His glory, unto all patience and long suffering with joyfulness; giving thanks to the Father, who made us meet for the share of the inheritance of the saints in light" (i. 10-12).

IN our last lecture we considered what may be designated as the source of the Christian's walk, in this we are to consider its processes, or more properly speaking perhaps, we are to learn in what that worthy walk consists.

Let it always be borne in mind, however, that this prayer of the apostle for a worthy walk was offered in behalf of Christians; for those who were already pardoned and accepted, and saved in Christ (i. 4, 5, 21, 22). Only those who *have been* reconciled to God through the blood of the cross can even start to lead a holy life; but all such are bound to do so, and are enabled therefor. The "thorough knowledge of God's will in all spiritual wisdom and

understanding" never fails to fill the soul with
the sense of this obligation, and supplies the
spirit and power of obedience.

1. To walk worthily of Christ is to be *bringing forth fruit in every good work*.   There
must be *fruit bearing*.   For Christ is the
Saviour *from sin* and *unto holiness* (Matt. i.
21 ; and Rom. vi.) ; and His salvation is as well
life as deliverance.

The fruit borne must be *good works*.   There
is a great variety of these.   All acts of worship : prayer, confession, praise, reading the
Word of God ; the doing good to the bodies
and souls of men : almsgiving, personal visit-
ing, earnest kindness, teaching, and guiding.
Especially, the Christian's own personal culture in all the Christian virtues and graces :
honesty, uprightness, truthfulness, the bridling
of the tongue, habitual purity of thought, tem-
perance, meekness, patience, gentleness, love,
joy, peace (I. Cor. xiii. 4-7; Gal. v. 22, 23;
II. Pet. i. 5-7, etc.).   The fruit-bearing must
be in every kind of good works.

Nay, in *every* good work of every kind.   Our
attention and interest must be concentrated on
each particular, according as its claims require.
Bible study, for instance, should be attended to,
at the same time that active beneficence is duly
honored ; neither should be neglected, but also

neither should be allowed to filch from the
other.   And so as to every one of all.   A tree
produces but one kind of fruit; a tree of gospel
righteousness all kinds.   And of this James
i. 27 is an apt illustration.

2. To walk worthily of Christ is to be *increasing by the thorough knowledge of God.*

That is, the Christian himself must be increasing.   At the same time of his bringing
forth fruit he should be himself personally enlarging.   In his perceptions of the truth, his
appreciations of "the fulness of the blessing of
the Gospel of peace"; in the exercise of his
affections, in his capacity of spiritual enjoyment, in spiritual wisdom and understanding;
and so, in the power of fruitfulness.   It is his
being filled with the thorough knowledge of
God that causes him to increase; and the more
he is filled, the more he enlarges.   According
as he takes in the truth, both understanding
and heart are expanded, and his moral power
is multiplied (Deut. xxxii. 2; Hos. xiv. 5, 6).
At the same time, the bringing forth fruit in
good works reacts upon us, helping to increase our spiritual wisdom and understanding; and this, in turn, increases ourselves personally.

3. To walk worthily of Christ is the being
strengthened with all strength, according to the

power of His glory, unto all patience and long suffering with joyfulness. For the Christian walk is in the midst of dangers, and trials, and toils; and we need to be continually strengthened. We need the strength of love, the strength of joy, the strength of peace, the strength of hope. When these things are in us and abound, they make us efficient for every good word and work.

This strengthening is from the Holy Spirit (Eph. iii. 16), who, as operating in us by means of the truth, gives us strength in connection with, and in the proportion of, our increasing by the knowledge of God. So that while this strengthening is not of our own producing, yet may we always have it as exercising our responsibility to know the truth, and to depend on the teachings of the Spirit. Since He alone strengthens, so we become strengthened according as we feel our weakness and dependence. And the more we are thus enabled by the Holy Spirit to increase in the knowledge of God, the more that knowledge itself deepens and develops this feeling of dependence; and, therefore, the more we avail ourselves by faith of the Spirit's ministry. And so we become stronger and stronger in that strength of love, and joy, and peace, and hope, of which the truth is so full. Strengthened with *all strength,* or, *every* strength. Just the strength which the particular duty may require.

Strengthened *unto all patience and long suffering.* These graces are universally necessary. With regard to what good work is it that we do not need to have them in exercise? Patience: quiet, unmurmuring, submissive endurance. Long suffering: the principle whence the other proceeds; long-mindedness, our thoughts and feelings being lengthened, as it were, as we increase in the knowledge of God. Patience: not cowardice or despondency. Long suffering: not wrath or revenge toward men, nor irritation toward God.

With joyfulness. Either strengthened *unto* joyfulness, as well as unto all patience and long suffering, or strengthened *with* joyfulness unto patience and long suffering. Either way joy itself is strength; and either way it is the pervading element of patience or long suffering. To be rejoicing in God is to be ready for whatever trials and toils. And always the thorough knowledge of God is productive of joy; for such knowledge precludes doubt and slavish fear, and fills the soul with the sweetness of personal assurance. Joyfulness is the peculiar glory of the Gospel. And since it is of the essence of strength, all-important it is to the efficiency of the Christian life (Rom. v. 3-5; Acts v. 41).

Strengthened thus *according to the power of His glory*. The power which is a part of God's glory; which belongs to His glory, or to that bright display of Himself in Christ and His Word. In Ephesians i. 19, 20 we have a statement of the power of His glory; the power whose working "He wrought in Christ, when He raised Him from the dead, and set Him at His own right hand in the heavenly places"; and according to the working of that mighty power "is the exceeding greatness of His power to usward who believe." What a standard and measure of the strengthening with which the Holy Ghost is ready to enrich us! How large-hearted should be our prayers! How receptive our faith!

Patience, Long Suffering, Joy! What a triad of blessedness! What richest fruits! What strongest strength! What excellencies of the Christian life!

4. To walk worthily of Christ is to be *giving thanks to the Father, who made us meet for the share of the inheritance of the saints in light*. This fourth particular crowns the whole of a holy life, and it pervades the whole. The rejoicings of assurance must run through all the duties and all the processes of the Christian life, if that life be efficient in a manner at all worthy of Christ as the Saviour. It must have

no slavishness in it. It must think, and feel, and act, in the freedom and confidence of conscious childhood. Oh, most blessed view of our worthy walk!

But this crowning and all-pervading element of a holy life is so full and rich, and of such importance is its being well understood, that we reserve it for a fuller treatment in the next chapter.

6

THE CHRISTIAN'S BLESSEDNESS

WHAT IT IS, AND HOW AND WHEN IT CAME

"Giving thanks to the Father, who made us meet for the share of the inheritance of the saints in light" (Col. i. 12).

THIS verse we had before us in the preceding chapter, in which Paul is heard to pray for the Colossian believers to be enabled to walk worthily of Christ, and is, in part, his statement of what constitutes such a walk. Having prayed for their "being filled with the thorough knowledge of God's will in all spiritual wisdom and understanding," as the source of a worthy Christian life, he further prays that they may accomplish such a life in four particulars: in *the bringing forth of fruit* in every good work; in the *increasing* by the thorough knowledge of God; in the being *strengthened with all strength,* according to the power of His glory, unto *all patience and longsuffering, with joyfulness;* and in *the giving of thanks* to the Father who *made them meet* for the share of the inheritance of the saints in light. The first three of these particulars we considered in the previous chapter, only glancing at the significance of the fourth. But this last element of a worthy Christian walk deserves to be thoroughly considered. It contains so remarkable a declaration of the believer's already perfected meetness for the inheritance in light, it so enforces upon him the duty of thankfully recognizing the fact, it so encompasses the Christian life with an atmosphere of joy and gladness, it is so rich in practical teachings for our lifelong contest with the powers of evil, we shall find it as sweet and refreshing as is "cold water to a thirsty soul."

1. The Christian's blessedness is an *inheritance*. It is something allotted, assigned; something conferred by right of position and relationship. It is not won by his own efforts, else it is not an inheritance. No righteousness of his own, no good works, no labors of his, have anything to do in the procuring of it for him. It follows BIRTH. He is *begotten* to an inheritance "incorruptible, and undefiled, that fadeth not away" (I. Peter i. 3, 4). The new birth and heirship are facts correlative and simultaneous. "If children, then heirs, heirs of God, and joint heirs with Christ" (Rom. viii. 17).

2. The Christian's blessedness is the inheritance of *saints*. It belongs to saints as such; to

all saints, and to none else. But who are
saints? They are those who have been sanctified (made saints) by the sprinkling of the
blood of Jesus Christ (Heb. x. 10). All believers in Christ, then, are saints; for every believer has been sprinkled with His blood, and
brought under its shelter and its endearing
value. Purged from guilt and condemnation,
invested with God's righteousness in Christ
(II. Cor. v. 21), and accepted of God, he is
also sanctified, set apart, by God's bloody mark
upon him, as His own jewel; is made sacred
and very dear to Him as His own *peculium,*
His own property (I. Cor. vi. 20; I. Peter ii. 9).
This is judicial sanctification, and it is perfect.
Out of it, and always according to the heart's
realization of it, comes *practical* sanctification.
But it is the judicial setting apart which makes
any one a saint; it is the sprinkling of the blood
which accomplishes this result; it is God's own
act, once done, which *saints* us, and in His own
calendar He hath written it.

3. The Christian's blessedness is the inheritance *in light.* This is its sphere, its seat, its
sweetness, its excellence, its glory. This word
LIGHT is the authoritative affirmation of what
we just now inferred as to the nature of the
inheritance. Light is the emblem of *truth, holiness, purity, perfection.* God is Light (I. John

i. 5). Christ is Light (Luke ii. 32). The Word of God is light (Ps. cxix. 105). The inheritance in light, then, is such a condition of blessedness as is constituted of the truth as it is in Jesus, as reflects Christ Himself, as shines with the splendors of God. There the true, the holy, the pure, and the perfect, are the constituent elements of things, and also the order of procedure.

Of course, this locates the inheritance in heaven. For where but there does light exist so absolutely? (Rev. xxi. 23, xxii. 5). As in Bonar's hymn—

"Sunshine is ever pure;
  No art of man can rob it of its beauty,
  Nor stain its unpolluted heavenliness;
  It is the fairest, purest thing in nature;
  Fit type of that fair heaven where all is pure,
  And into which no evil thing can enter,
  Where darkness comes not, where no shadow falls,
  Where night and sin can have no dwelling place."

And yet this does not *confine* the inheritance to heaven; for saints are now in light, and are light. "They have been called out of darkness into His marvelous light" (I. Peter ii. 9), and are now "the children of light, and the children of the day" (I. Thess. v. 5). The inheritance, then, is located here and now, as well as there and then. In the next verse to our text, as explanatory of the being made meet for the inheritance in light, it is said that "God delivered us out of the power of darkness, and translated us into the kingdom of His dear Son, in whom we have redemption, the forgiveness of sins." So that, as saints, we are already in light and in the kingdom. We enjoy the inheritance even now; not the whole of it, indeed, but in part. *Born* of God, at once we *believe on* Christ, and are pardoned, and accepted, and sanctified, and made dear to God; and therein we have come to the inheritance, for straightway we have fellowship with God, and He has become our conscious good and satisfaction, and the peace of God and joy in the Holy Ghost are as the feelings of the heir to an estate, when he has come to his majority, and has been actually installed in possession. We are just what the truth, as it is in Jesus, has made us; and we are holy to God, under His own estimation of the value of the blood; and we are perfect in the perfection of Christ (Col. ii. 10); and we purify ourselves even as He is pure (I. John iii. 3). It is the inheritance enjoyed even here; imperfectly, indeed, and with many disturbances and with heart-longings for the heavenly circumstances of possession. But it is the inheritance. So that not only have we heaven in prospect, but also an earnest of heaven, a very part of heaven already.

4. The Christian's blessedness is an inheritance *that is shared.* "Meet," says the text, "for *the share* of the inheritance of the saints in light." All are equally heirs, equally born of God, equally pardoned and justified in Christ our Righteousness, equally sanctified by the blood, equally put in possession here, and shall be equally put in possession there; and to all belong the same inheritance, the same fellowship with God, the same conscious satisfaction in God, the same peace of God, and joy in the Holy Ghost. Yet each his own. *"The share."* Differences and degrees exist both there and here. In the one body are many members, and all the members are but one body; yet the foot is not the hand, the nose is not the eye. To every man "according to his several ability." Fellowship with God here may differ, in certain regards, in different saints, although they be equally faithful. One may be a Paul, another an Epaphras; both holding the same truths, having the same life, feeling the same joy in God; but the one sees farther, thinks deeper, lives wider, than the other; the one is as the eagle, bathing its wings in the sunshine of the open heavens, the other as the canary, in a smaller sphere, which yet it fills with song and joyance.

Besides, there are differences in faithfulness

among saints, and these lead to differently developed capacities of appreciation and enjoyment; and the latter differences require different degrees of advancement and employment in God's appointments concerning us. The saint who uses faithfully his opportunities for being filled with the thorough knowledge of God's will, becomes constantly self-enlarged, and so is constantly gaining as regards his present share of the inheritance, and also as regards his future share in heaven; for while each one there shall receive the crown of life (Rev. ii. 10), yet some crowns will have more stars in them than will others (Dan. xii. 3). Our blessedness is strictly an inheritance; and yet our Father, in a way wholly of grace, not at all of debt, may distinguish between His beloved children, the recipients of the same inheritance.

5. The Christian's blessedness is an inheritance for which the Father hath made us meet.

A meetness or fitness for it we do need to have. A sick man cannot partake of a sumptuous feast; neither could we share in this inheritance and enjoy God as our souls' satisfaction, sinners as we are, corrupt, guilty and condemned, except as having received a new man in the being born again, and thus having been brought into sympathy with God, and as having been pardoned and accepted of God and made dear to Him in Christ our Righteousness. These results of the work of the Saviour are what constitutes His salvation, and He wrought them out for us, on purpose to "bring us to God," to make us *"heirs* of God," to secure to us the inheritance. Therefore it is the believing on the Lord Jesus Christ which makes us meet for the inheritance, for it is that which expresses the new birth, and at the same time receives the righteousness wherein we are justified and sanctified to God. Of the same import is the expression in the text, "The *Father* made us meet"; that is, as the next verse shows, the Father of Christ. God made us meet, then, in His character as the Father of Christ; in other words, He did it *because of, and by means of,* the work of Christ in us.

Hence it follows, that the making us meet for the inheritance is an act of God done and finished for us once in the time past. When a soul is new-born it becomes so in a moment of time; and then, believing on Christ, instantly it is completely pardoned, completely justified and completely sanctified in the infinite value of the blood of the Son of God. Wherefore we are made meet for the inheritance, not by a progressive process, but by an act of God instantly done and finished.

There can be no greater acceptance of us in
heaven than God gives us now in Christ, for
even there we shall stand accepted in Him
alone. Our Father will not more fully rejoice
over us there than He does here; for then, as
now, He will see us only as in Christ. Our
meetness, then, for the one part of the inheritance is just our meetness for the other part.
And so, when some eminent saint comes to his
death-bed, what is it that gives him his comfort, his serene triumph, in that critical hour?
Is it his progressive practical sanctification?
Indeed, no. He is too conscious of many failures, that he should rely on that as his passport
through the gates into the city. Thankful he
is to God, that He has enabled him to serve
Him with whatever degree of faithfulness, and
he may speak of it to the praise of the glory
of His grace; but he rests not his destination
on so imperfect a prop as that. What is it
then? Just this: the infinite value of the blood
which sprinkled him. On that he rests, as on
the Rock of Ages. Yes, Christ Himself is
our only meetness for the inheritance, and our
believing on Christ is our having the meetness.

And can the intelligent heart hesitate as to its
absolute repose on meetness like this? The
phrase "made meet" is just one word in the
Greek; and in the adjective form it was used

by the Lord, when, in answer to the offer of two swords by the disciples, He said, *"It is enough";* and by the Apostle Paul, when he said, "Who is *sufficient* for these things?" (Luke xii. 38; II. Cor. ii. 16.) Christ, as our meetness for the inheritance, is enough, sufficient, complete. The common phrase, "ripening for heaven" is false, except as regards a larger capacity of enjoyment and higher degrees of blessedness. The believer *was* made meet in Christ; made enough, sufficient, complete.

Two practical observations may fittingly close this theme. (1) We should recognize and enjoy the fact of this already accomplished meetness. *"Giving thanks* to the Father who made us meet." Distinctly apprehending the fact, appropriating it and praising God for it. Here is *assurance;* the assurance of understanding, the assurance of faith, the assurance of hope.

And this is the very prayer of the apostle. He beseeches God to enable the Colossian believers to see and appreciate it, and to rejoice in it. What present joy and peace are our positive allotments from God! Nor is it presumption in us, when thus we believe God and glorify Christ. It is obedience; it is humility; it is self-renunciation; it is sinking out of ourselves and rising in the Saviour.

(2) This assurance is a necessary part of our walking worthily of Christ.

Remember the connection. The apostle is speaking of what constitutes a worthy walk; and in order to get it he prays that the assurance of an already perfected meetness for the inheritance may fill the soul with its joy and peace.

7

THE CHRISTIAN'S DELIVERANCE

WHENCE, WHERE AND HOW

"Who delivered us out of the power of darkness, and translated us into the kingdom of the Son of His love; in whom we have the redemption, the forgiveness of sins" (i. 13, 14).

PROPERLY considered the apostle's prayer ended with the twelfth verse, and now he glides from the prayer into the subject matter of the epistle, the Person, work and glory of Christ. At the same time, the thirteenth verse is in apposition with the twelfth, and explains the nature of the "meetness" which the Father hath given us for "the inheritance of the saints in light." In the same way the fourteenth verse is in apposition with the thirteenth and explains the "deliverance" which we have received.

Bearing in mind that the apostle is speaking of true believers in Christ, if we are such, he says three things of us:

1. The Father hath delivered us out of the power of darkness.

Darkness is in Scripture the image of **sin,** and ignorance, and falsehood. "Men love darkness rather than light, because their deeds are evil," said Jesus Christ (John ii. 19). To "cast off the works of darkness" is to cast off sins (Rom. xii. 12). The hating one's brother is the walking in darkness (I. John ii. 11). Not to have fellowship with God is to walk in darkness (I. John i. 6). Thus darkness is ungodliness, estrangement from God, opposition to God; and all those dreadful evils which are involved in such a state of heart and mind.

"The power of darkness" is a frightful expression. How much it is capable of meaning may be seen in Romans i. 21-32. But we may also get a shocking idea of its significance by looking around us; for we shall see the abounding of ignorance of the things of God, of profanity, of uncleanness and lasciviousness, of gluttony and drunkenness, of hatred and malice. Nay, we need not confine our view to those divisions of human society which are lowest down. In the more refined and cultured circles, what pride and vanity, what self-conceit, what secret sins, what enmity to God, and again and again, what outbreaks of crime! The power of sin, the tyranny of error, the slavery of corruption;

these things are everywhere, and are the characteristics of human nature.

Every believer in Christ has been delivered
out of the power of darkness. That is to say,
he was wholly within its power, absolutely
subjected to it; and was himself helpless.
"That which is born of the flesh is flesh" (John
iii. 6), and "the mind of the flesh is enmity
against God; it is not subjected to the law of
God, neither indeed can be" (Rom. viii. 7).
And it is led captive by the devil at his will
(II. Tim. ii. 26). So that no man cometh
to Christ except the Father draw him (John
vi. 44). It is a divine deliverance, whenever
it takes place. God alone can remove us from
within the power of darkness.

Such a deliverance must be effected, in part,
by means of a new birth from God; by His
begetting in us an essentially new life. Only
"that which is born of the Spirit is spirit"
(John iii. 6), and only they who are according
to the Spirit of God do mind the things of the
Spirit (Rom. viii. 5). Only such a new life,
so essentially new that it exists alone by means
of a birth, and is therefore so diverse in kind
from the life of flesh, can feel sympathy with
the pure and blessed things of God, and is able
to crush out of the way the fascinations of
corruption. The gift from God of such a life

is indeed the being removed from within the
power of darkness. And it is that drawing to
Christ, of which He spake as being so indis-
pensable that the Father should do, in order
that any one might come to Him.

Now, this deliverance, in every occurrence
of it, is effected completely, and at once. The
Father *delivered* us from the power of darkness. Observe the apostle's tense (aorist),
which expresses a certain definite past time.
He does not even use the perfect tense, and
say, "The Father has delivered us"; although
that would be true. But his purpose was to
fix attention on a past moment, when the deliverance was effected absolutely and finished-
ly. The Father *did* deliver us. When? At
the moment of the new birth, and of faith in
Christ. Then the new life was wholly given;
at the first indeed, the life of an infant in
Christ, nevertheless, a complete life. And
then, the pardon bestowed had reference to
every sin, and swept off the last vestige of condemnation. There is no progress in this deliverance; it springs forth full-formed, and on
the instant. We dishonor God's work, and we
dishonor God's word, if, as believers in Christ,
we are thinking *longingly* of the deliverance;
as though it had not been already, or had been
only partially. In every prayer, in every duty,

in every condition, we are to act as being assured of its past accomplishment; only we
confess our daily sins, just as beloved children
ever do, and are daily forgiven, as children ever
are. But that forgiveness of sins, which means
the taking away of condemnation, is to the
Christian an act of God already done and finished.

The *Father* delivered us. He, then, is not
withdrawn at an infinite distance from us, as
the false teachers at Colossæ suggested. He
has an active, minute, loving, efficient, infallible, personal interest in the deliverance of
every believer in Christ. He who inhabiteth
eternity turns His infinite heart to the poorest,
the obscurest, the wretchedest sinner, and on
that single point of sin and guilt lavishes the
energies of His love.

2. Having thus delivered us, the Father hath
translated us into the kingdom of the Son of
His love.

Removed from a place is one thing, settle-
ment in another place is quite another thing.
Deliverance out of the power of darkness and
translation into the kingdom, though inseparable blessings, are yet distinct. Both are equally
important and both are secured. God will have
no deficiency in His salvation of the believer.
The Father did deliver us (aorist tense) out of

the power of darkness, and He did translate us
(aorist again) into the kingdom.

The kingdom of Christ, therefore, exists now
and here. The manifested state or form of this
kingdom is called in Scripture "the kingdom in
the heavens" (Rom. viii. 19; Matt. viii. 11),
but that and this are one and the same kingdom. *That* is yet to be; meanwhile this *is* that,
as regards principles and constitution. The
only difference is one of external circumstances.

The kingdom of Christ on earth is spoken
of as though it were conterminous with the
visible Church; as in the parable of the wheat
and the tares (Matt. xiii. 24). But the very
places where this is done do themselves show
that the whole of the visible church is not the
kingdom of Christ; for tares are not wheat,
and are yet to be gathered together and burned.
Rather, the true kingdom of Christ here is
within the visible church; "a wheel within a
wheel." It consists of all those, and only those,
who have been really delivered out of the
power of darkness. Into this inner community
within the visible Church the Father translates
every one to whom He has given the new life,
and who has received, by faith in Jesus Christ,
the forgiveness of sins; and he becomes a member, not alone of the visible Church, but of the

Church spiritual; of the kingdom which is righteousness, and peace and joy in the Holy Ghost (Rom. xiv. 17).

It is the kingdom of the Father's Son. Not of angels, as the false teachers taught (Col. ii. 18), but of Him who has the inheritance; the Only Begotten of the Father. But we, as having been delivered out of the power of darkness, are made sons of God in Him, the Father's Son, and are joint heirs with Him (Rom. viii. 17). We have the same inheritance. Our place in the kingdom is by right of sonship. A kingdom of God's dear children; partakers of the divine nature (II. Peter i. 4); embodiments of the graces and beauties of the Father's Spirit in the heart (Gal. v. 22, 23). A kingdom of paternal power and sweetness, and of filial communion and joy.

It is the kingdom of the Son of the Father's love. Love is the essence of the Father's being (I. John iv. 16); and since the Son is the Begotten of the Father, He, the King, is of the essence of the Father, and is also love. Thus, what a transfusion of the blessedness of the Godhead throughout the kingdom! A kingdom of love! The King on His throne is love; the subjects of the throne are recipients of love; and God is that love!

The translation, then, was from the tyranny

of sin and guilt into the freedom and the settledness of the sovereignty of love; from the
slavery of evil into citizenship in light and
glory; from mere earthiness into full sympathy
with God. Such *was the* Father's act of translation; but hereafter it will prove to have lifted
the believers even into a co-enthronement with
Christ, as a ruler in the kingdom of divine love
(Rev. iii. 21).

3. The Father so delivered us, and translated us, only in Christ, in whom we have the
redemption, the forgiveness of sins.   This
verse of our text simply gives us the ground
of all we have been saying.

The apostle calls it "the redemption."   It
was that which had been prophesied of; which
was the same as the deliverance from the
power of darkness mentioned in the verse before; which was one with the forgiveness of
sins.

This redemption we have in Christ. Apart
from Him it does not exist; in Him it is both
exemplified and impersonated. The Father laid
upon Him our sins, and He bare the punishment of them. He paid the price of His own
blood and sufferings, and thereby He was
Himself delivered from the awful burden which
He had taken upon Him. His own deliverance, His own redemption, is ours, who be-

lieve on Him; for He was in our place. In
receiving Him, therefore, we receive the redemption; and as His own deliverance was actual and complete, so is ours. It is positively
the forgiveness of sins.

It is not "the passing by" (Rom. iii. 25) of
sins, but real remission. It is not the Romish
remission of guilt, while yet not of punishment, and hence their Purgatory. But "there is
therefore now no condemnation to them who
are in Christ Jesus" (Rom. vii. 1). Absolutely and completely the sins are forgiven. The
Father did cast them all "into the depths of
the sea" (Mic. vii. 19). Nor do we need any
penances, or satisfactions of our own; nor any
efforts of self-righteousness, which is no righteousness. The Lord Jesus Christ wrought out
the redemption in His own person, and, receiving Him by faith, we receive His own personal deliverance in all its reality and all its
fulness.

How demonstrably our text confirms the
teaching of the preceding twelfth verse, as regards the already accomplished " meetness " of
the believer for the inheritance in light. In
this joy of the Lord let us consecrate ourselves
to His blessed service.

8

CHRIST IN RELATION TO CREATION

"Who is the image of God the invisible, the First-born of all creation; because in Him was created the universe, things in the heavens and things on the earth, things visible and things invisible, whether thrones, whether dominions, whether principalities, whether powers; the universe has been created by Him and unto Him. And He Himself is before all things, and in Him the universe consists" (i. 15-17).

WE have now arrived at the subject of the epistle, the Person and the Glory of Christ. At the very threshold the apostle meets and sweeps away all those Gnostic teachings which were beginning to be left in the Church at Colossæ. Christ, the only Mediator between God and the Creation, and between God and sinful men, is Himself the very fulness of the Deity. Away, then, with those Gnostic angelic emanations from the Godhead, which were regarded as only *more or less divine,* and which, for that especial reason, were held to be the only fitting links of intercourse between God and the universe. Both the Gnostic cosmogony and the Gnostic religion

were shattered to pieces by this true doctrine
of the Person of Christ. And the apostle an-
nounces his subject in a most comforting connection; for he has mounted up to this high
argument from the stepping-stone of the fourteenth verse, wherein he had declared that it is
in Christ we have redemption, the forgiveness
of sins. So that whatever of majesty and glory
is predicted of Christ in this statement of the
subject, it all reflects back on that declaration,
and is the demonstration of its truth and preciousness.

In these verses (15-20) we have one of the
great passages of the New Testament. As a
Christological statement, it has scarcely an
equal, certainly no superior. Compare Col. ii.
9-15; Eph. i. 20-23; Phil. ii. 6-11; Heb. i.
2-14. Christ is presented, first, in His relation
to Creation (15-17), and, secondly, in His relation to the Church (18-20).

We have now before us His relation to creation, or, as it might be stated, His relation to
God as the foundation of His relation to creation. *"He is the image of God the invisible, the
First-Born of all creation."*

The image of God the invisible. An image
(*eikon*) is, of course, a likeness (*homoioma*),
but while these two Greek words might be used
in many cases indifferently, in many others not

so. Every image is a likeness, but every likeness is not an image. The following illustrations have been frequently given: Two eggs
are like each other, but, neither of the two being derived from the other, neither is the image
of the other. Two men are alike, who yet are
not akin: the one is not the image of the other.
But the head on a coin is not only a likeness,
it is the image of the sovereign. It is *derived*
from the sovereign, and it is a *representation* of
him. In a word, it is a *copy* of the sovereign. So, the sun's reflection in water.
And so, a child: he is not only the
likeness but also the image of his father. Such is the distinction between the two
Greek words above mentioned. An image,
then, besides being a likeness, contains the facts
of *derivation* and *representation*. It is a copy.
So that Christ is here declared to be the copy
of the Father; the *representation* of Him, because *derived* from Him. He is "the *brightness* of His glory, and the character, the *exact
impress,* of His person" (Heb. i. 3). "In Him
dwelleth all the fullness of the Godhead" (Col.
ii. 9). "Being in the *form* of God, He thought
it not robbery to be *equal* with God" (Phil. ii.
6). *Derived* from Him, He is both *likeness*
and *representation;* the exact copy of God.

It will thus be seen that this word "image,"

as applied to Christ, is the expression of His Sonship to the Father, seeing that the Scriptures describe His derivation as being that of a son from his father. Nay, it is the expression of His *Eternal Sonship,* since, as we shall see hereafter, our text speaks of Him as the image of God *prior* to the creation of all things.

In this word "image," then, as applied to Christ, we have these three teachings: He is *the Son* of God, He is the *Eternal* Son of God, He is *God.* And assurance is made doubly sure by what is said of this Image of God in the after words of our text: that "in Him, and by Him, and unto Him, the universe was created."

As the image of God, He is God; even as the son of a man is man. But as the image of the Father, He is not the Father; even as a man's son is not himself. The person of Christ is distinct from the person of the Father; yet there is only one God. Godhead is not constituted of Deity alone; but of Deity *as it is in certain inter-relations.* Those relations are *within* the one Godhead; but, as relations, they *difference* the Son from the Father; therefore may the one be the image of the other.

And now there is another great idea in this word "image" as here connected; it carries the idea of *manifestation.* "The image of the *in-*

visible": the manifestion of Him who is invisible. God is invisible as regards, not alone our bodily eyes, but as well our inward eye, our comprehension. In this sense He is invisible to all creature intelligences, howsoever lofty; for finiteness cannot embrace infiniteness. The Eternal Son is the manifestation of God to all intelligences of the universe.

Accordingly, "image" is here suggestive of another expression, the *logos,* the word (John i. 1). He is the Word of God: God's *purpose and expression,* God's *Personal Word,* His Personal purpose and expression. The Eternal Son is the manifestation of God.

It is this idea of manifestation which makes the phrase, "the image of God," as applied to Christ, so exceedingly precious. It is the fact of Him being God's Personal expression of Himself which gives us all our interest in Christ. Without this fact, there were no redemption in Him, and no satisfaction for our souls. On the other hand, that He is *such* an expression of God; that He is the Son, the Eternal Son, God; *this* is to us the fullness of truth, and "unsearchable riches of grace."

But does the apostle here refer to the Incarnation? Does he mean to say that the Son is the image of God the invisible, by reason of His having been made flesh? He does *not* mean to say this, for, as our 16th verse shows, he is speaking of the Son as being the image of God *prior to all creation.* In this phrase he does not refer to the Incarnation; but to the essential relations in the Deity: the Eternal Fatherhood to the Son, the Eternal Sonship to the Father, the Eternal Word, the Eternal Image.

At the same time, true it is, that the Son as incarnate was and is the image of God. "He that hath seen Me hath seen the Father," said Jesus (John xiv. 9). Only so, however, because of His being the *eternal* image. It was not the incarnation which made Him the image of God; but it brought Him, as being that image within our grasp. Now it was for the sake of our appreciating Him in His incarnate condition that the apostle here speaks of Him in His eternal relations. Hence it follows that, although He does not here refer to the incarnation, he yet means that it shall be here suggested to us (compare 14th verse), and that we shall especially learn the lesson of our absolute dependence on Christ for knowing God at all. He is the image of God to us only because He is essentially and eternally His image. Therefore, except we see God as imaged forth in Him, we do not properly see God at all. The imaginings of men cannot bring God into view;

for their imaginings are merely their own *image-makings,* and men's ideal images of the infinite God are as inadequate as are the stone images of heathen peoples. Neither can creation bring God into view if looked at apart from Christ; for although the general facts of divine causation, and wisdom, and power, are evidenced in creation, they do but *tell* us that God is, rather than *show* Him to us. We cannot know God except as in Christ, who is the brightness of His glory, any more than one can see a lighted candle except in the rays which come from it to the eye. What God should be to us practically, and what may be His will concerning us; all this we can know only as we *touch* Him *in Jesus Christ.*

The apostle, however, is directly speaking of the Son as being the image of the Father *before the Incarnation.* "The image of God the invisible"; of Him who was then invisible. It follows that, before His Incarnation, He was the manifestation of the Father to the angels. They knew God, and they know God, only by means of the Son. They cannot properly get hold of ideas of Him, except as the Son shall reveal Him to them. He is invisible to their mental eyes, except as being visible in His Image, His own Filial Image.

Yet how is it that the eternal Son is less in-

comprehensible than the eternal Father? He
is equally God with the Father; and they two,
with the Holy Ghost, are one God. How is
the Son the manifestation of the Father any
more than the Father is of the Son? Or than
the Holy Ghost is the manifestation of both?
The Son, as God, must be Himself the invisible. Unquestionably. He is not less incomprehensible than the Father. Now, on the sup-
position that God is to be made known at all,
either the adorable, incomprehensible Three
must all become the united revealers of the one
Godhead, or else some one, or two, of the three
must have this office. All we can say is, it is
simply the eternal will of the Godhead that the
Son is the Revealer. Doubtless either the
Father or the Spirit *could* be it, but not so was
it willed. And we can see what strikes us as
an evident propriety in this arrangement. For
the Son, as such, deriving by an eternal gener-
ation, is the essential image or representation
of the Father. But the Father is not the image
of the Son. It would seem, therefore, to be
eminently fitting that He who is the Begotten
representation of Godhead should be the manifestation of the Godhead to the creation. At
any rate, so it is. The Son of God is the Revealer, at once, of the Father, and of the Son,
and of the Holy Ghost. We receive the fact
and we enjoy the blessedness of it.

9

CHRIST IN RELATION TO THE CHURCH

"And He Himself is the Head of the body, the Church; who is the Beginning, the First-born from among the dead, in order that He might become in all things Himself pre-eminent" (i. 18).

THE apostle is still engaged with the announcement of his subject. Having made his statement of the Person and Glory of Christ as regards creation (15-17), he now makes it as regards the Church. And notice that Christ's relation to the Church is the projection of His relation to creation. The statement of the one follows after that of the other and results from it. It is simply His relation to creation carried forward. He Himself is the Head of the body, the Church, i.e., the very same who (as the preceding verse said) is before all things, and in whom the universe consists.

Thus there is an absolute unity of origin in creation and redemption. There is not, as the Gnostic teachers supposed, an opposition, a conflict between creative power and redeeming purposes. Redemption was not meant to be a remedy for the failure of creation. The latter was not the work of an imperfect being, or beings, and to be regarded as essentially evil; nor is the former defective and to be pieced out by man's devices. The one Mediator between God and all creation is Christ, the Image of God the invisible, the eternal *Logos,* the manifestation of Deity; and the very same is the one Mediator in spiritual things. Thus the true doctrine of Christ's person was the confutation of the Gnostic cosmogony, that the universe was created by certain angelic emanations from the Deity, who were more or less imperfect, according to the degree of their remove from Him, and hence, that matter is inherently evil; and also it was the confutation of the Gnostic religion, that man must make himself holy by means of various ordinances of abstinence from contact with material things, and thus complete the work of redemption. Whether in creation or in redemption, Jesus Christ is the absolute and all-perfect expression of God.

1. The nature of His relation to the Church. *"He Himself is the Head of the body, the Church."*

Himself, in whom was created the universe,

and in whom it consists, and no other, is the
Head of the Church. This was aimed, perhaps, at some falsely imagined head in the doctrine of the false teachers. A demolishing
stroke as regards the Papacy. "Body" and
"Church" are in apposition. The body *which
is* the Church (Col. i. 24).

The Church (*ecclesia*); an assembly *called
out.* The Church here referred to is the whole
number of true believers in Christ; those whom
the apostle calls "the saints, and the faithful
in Christ Jesus," and of whom he says, "God
chose them in Christ before the foundation of
the world" (Eph. i. 1-4), and whom God has
called out of the world by regeneration and
conversion; by giving them new hearts, and
leading them to believe on the Lord Jesus
Christ. Only to such is Christ the *vital* Head;
for although He be professedly the Head to
merely nominal Christians, yet is He not really
so.

This Church is the *body* of Christ. As a
body, it has organic unity; as much so as the
visible cosmos. Its internal relations are not
tangible to the senses, but not less real are its
order, harmony, and ultimate purpose. And as
the body of Christ, it is one with Him in life,
in position, in strength, in glory. This vital
oneness with Him is something tremendous.

The Church is so new-created as to have been made the living body of its Creator.

For, of this Church, His body, Christ is the Head. Not merely the Governmental head, "head over all things to the Church" (Eph. i. 22), but the *vital* head as well, since that of which He is the Head is His body, which, "by joints and bands having nourishment ministered, and knit together, increaseth with the increase of God" (Col. ii. 19). Jesus Christ is the Sovereign Lord of all creation, and as such He does and will govern for the benefit of His Church; but, additionally, He is the Head of it as His own body; the seat of its life, the source of its activity, the center of its unity, the inspiring, ruling, guiding, sustaining power of its spiritual being and blessedness.

Thus His relation to the Church is the exact parallel of that which He sustains to the universe. It is the parallel; a relation distinct from that other, but of equal creative power, and an equal sovereign Lordship. At the same time it is a deeper truth; a truth *within* that of His relation to the physical worlds, and which could not be a truth except as grounded in His Lordship of all creation, and as being the crown and glory of the universe of things. It is an *imperium in imperio;* but He is the one Sovereign of both, and governs both for the consummation of this one of the two. He, in whom was created the universe, and in whom it consists, is the Head of His body, the Church, the new creation, for the purpose of causing it to "grow up into Him," and to "come, in the unity of the faith, and of the knowledge of the Son of God, unto the measure of the stature of the fulness of Himself" (Eph. iv. 13-15), and for the purpose of ultimately "making all things new," assimilating all creation to the glory of His body, the Church (Rom. viii. 19-21; Rev. xxi. 5).

2. The accomplishment of this relation. "He Himself is the head of the body, the Church, *who is the beginning, the first-born from among the dead.*"

"Who" has here an argumentative force, equivalent to *in that He,* or *seeing that He,* is the beginning, etc. His headship of the Church has been made a *fact,* in that He has become the beginning, the first-born from among the dead. He was not this Head till then. As He was not Creator of the universe till creation was effected, although He was eternally the image of God, and by right of inheritance the Sovereign Lord of creation whenever it should have been effected, so He was not Head of the Church till He had become the beginning, the first-born from among the dead, although He was eternally designated thereto.

The two expressions, "the beginning" and "the first-born from among the dead," are in apposition. The beginning of what? Not of time, nor of creation (though both are true, sixteenth verse), but of that which may be required by the phrase, "the first-born from among the dead."

It is the fact of His *resurrection* which is here declared: He was "from among the dead." And was the *first* who ever rose in the true resurrection body: "Christ the first-fruits; afterward they that are Christ's at His coming" (I. Cor. xv. 23). He was the first, therefore, who was ever *born* from the dead. His humanity underwent, in this regard, a new birth; for, although He never had sin, yet He had "the *likeness* of sinful flesh." When He rose from the dead all this was changed, and He came forth in the power of resurrection life. He became God's first-born in resurrection, and therein was entitled to that "excellency of dignity and excellency of power" belonging to the first-born. He came forth in the fulness of the power and glory of redemption. Accordingly, He was the first-born *from among* the dead; from among all those who, because He rose, should also themselves rise: that is, from among His own people. For although all mankind shall rise in their bodies, yet they will not all rise in the resurrection body of the fifteenth chapter of I. Corinthians, nor will they all rise by reason of His rising; but to His own people His rising from the dead is the power and pledge of their rising in bodies like His own, and so He is the first-born *from among* the dead.

And now mark a difference. By reason of His being the Eternal Image of God, He became the beginning of all creation by simply speaking the creative word; whereas, although He is the Eternal Image of God, He became the beginning of the *new* creation only by becoming Himself Incarnate, by dying, and by rising again. What an emphasis has thus been placed on the magnitude and the transcendent glory, as compared with creation, of the work of REDEMPTION.

3. The aim and purpose of this relation. *"In order that He might become, in all things, Himself pre-eminent."*

"In order that." The design is most expressly stated. As He *is* first (seventeenth verse) with respect to all creation, so should He *become* first with respect to the Church. This was God's design in so constituting Him the Redeemer (Phil. ii. 6-11). He should become pre-eminent *in all things*. Everywhere and in all regards. As well in the Church as

in the universe; as in the heavens, so on the
earth; as in material things, so in spiritual; as
among the angels, so among men. He has the
pre-eminence by reason of His relation to creation; but now, also, an added pre-eminence.
Redemption is a loftier exhibition of the Eternal Son. Incarnation, Death and Resurrection, are an intenser display of the glories of
Deity.

He *Himself* should be pre-eminent. Precisely He is the objective point in the whole
plan. As creation is *unto* Him (sixteenth
verse), so redemption should *terminate in Him.*
All its processes and all its results should be
gauged and characterized by the unfolding of
the ineffable riches of His Eternal Sonship.
The purpose of redemption is the salvation of
us sinners; but the ultimate purpose is the
setting forth of the Redeemer Himself. In
this fuller display of Him who is the Son and
the manifestation of Deity, the inseparable
glory of the entire Godhead is made known;
and thus, all the more perfect and soul-satisfy-
ing and endlessly precious, and glorious for
ourselves, is our salvation, because of its being
the leading and ultimate purpose thereof to un-
veil before us the effulgent majesty of Him
who saves us.

He should be *pre-eminent.* That first rank,

that chiefest place, that brightest splendor, that everlasting and universally conceded divine Supremacy; how much does it all mean? Nothing shall there ever be to obscure Him. In creation, in providence, in redemption; in personal dignity, in excellence, in majesty, in love, in sweetness, in wisdom, in power, in preciousness; through "all the generations of the age of ages," always and everywhere, pre-eminent, supreme, first, chiefest, absolute, ineffable. And to such a one, even to Him, His saved ones shall be forever and forever united, even as a body is *livingly* one with its head.

To honor the Son in both creation and redemption is the Deity's darling thought. The reciprocal loves of the Eternal Three, in the eternal ages before creation, now find their historical expression in the progress of this design. Hence, the more simply and fully that we sinners come to the Incarnate Son, the harder we lean upon Him, the more we appropriate Him as our own, the deeper we go to pleasure ourselves in thinking of Him, and of how He has enriched us, so much the more we are of one mind with Deity, and ourselves are strains of joy in the divine harmony of all things.

"The sting of death is sin," says the apostle. It is no less the sting of life. It cannot be removed by any materialistic philosophy or by any socialistic enthusiasm. Christ alone cleanses, renews and gives the Spirit that makes all sin hateful and painful. In fellowship with Christ, the most seductive of forbidden paths have an odor like that of the valley of Hamon-gog.

If Joseph and Nicodemus had been half as devoted to Christ while He was living as they were when He was dead, how they could have helped and cheered Him and mightily wrought upon the lives of others!

10

CHRIST IN RELATION TO CREATION AND THE CHURCH

HIS DEITY—HIS WORK OF RECONCILIATION— ITS NATURE AND SCOPE

"Because in Him He [God] was pleased that the whole fulness should dwell, and by Him to reconcile the all things to Himself, having made peace through the blood of His cross; by Him, whether the things on the earth, whether the things in the heavens" (i. 19, 20).

IN these verses the apostle concludes his statement of the subject of the epistle, which is throughout that of the Person and Glory of Christ. First we have His relation to creation (5-17), then to the Church (18), and now to the Church again, only with reference to a further and special relation to creation as included in that of the Church.

Our text speaks of the work of reconciliation effected through the blood of the cross. This concerns, of course, the Church; but it is also referred to here as having to do with creation, "whether the things on the earth, whether the

things in the heavens." Thus, not only is the
Lord Jesus Christ the Creator of the universe
(16), but, by the blood of His cross, He sustains to it a further and special relation. It
was only as being the Creator that He could
become the Head of the Church; and now, as
being the Head of the Church, He reacts upon
creation. Of His two titles, the Creator, and
the Head of the Church, the loftier is the
latter.

Notice the inseparable connection between
the dwelling in Him of all the fulness and His
being the means of reconciling things to God
though the blood of His Cross. "God was
pleased that in Him all the fulness should
dwell, *and* by Him to reconcile, etc." His
ability to effect the reconciliation is made to
result from the dwelling of the fullness in Him.
This "fullness," as we shall presently see, is
that of Deity. He reconciles nothing to God,
save as He is Himself God.

Our text is like a prism; you may look
through it on several sides, and while seeing
every time the same one object, the Person and
glory of Christ, you yet behold it in many and
delightful colorings :—

1. *God was pleased that in Him the whole
fullness should dwell.*

In the sixteenth and seventeenth verses the

phrase "in Him" is equal to *in the Pre-incar-
nate Son*. Here it is the same as *in the Incarnate Son* (see the eighteenth verse). It is
Jesus, the Christ, who is in-dwelt by "the whole
fullness." This the apostle states emphatically; for, having spoken of the Son of God as
Incarnate ("the first-born from among the
dead"), he places the phrase "in Him" at *the
beginning* of the next sentence, thus making it
emphatic by position. In Jesus, the virgin-
born, the Son of Man, the Son of God, dwelt
and dwells the whole fullness.

The fullness of what? Of *the Godhead, of
Deity*. The connection of our text with the
16th and 17th verses demonstrates this to be
the meaning. Besides, in the 9th verse of the
second chapter of this epistle the apostle expressly says, "In Him dwelleth all the fullness
of the Godhead bodily." Now this word "fullness" means *the entire number, the entire
measure, the plenitude, the perfection*. In Him,
then, is the entire number, the plenitude, the
perfection of the attributes and energies of
Deity. Nay, there is almost a tautology in the
apostle's expression, "the whole fullness," or
"all the fullness"; very nearly as if he had said,
the full fullness. Jesus Christ is the Exhaus-
tion of Deity. How superlative is this statement of the Incarnation of God! See also
John i. 1-3, 14.

Although in Colossians ii. 9, as we have seen,
the apostle explains what fullness he refers to,
here he simply says "*the* fullness." Evidently
this word (*pleroma*) had already received a
definite theological import, and was in common
use among the philosophical religionists. As a
matter of fact, we know that the Gnostic
teachers did use it, and that they meant by it
the absolute perfection of Deity. But they
taught that only a fragment of it was given to
the various Divine Emanations or Angels, who,
according to their philosophy, were generated
from the Supreme Deity, and that the fragment became less and less in the proportion
that any one of those Emanations, in the suc-
cessions of the angelic chain, was removed
from the Deity. The apostle takes their own
word, and wresting it from such perversion,
appropriates it to Jesus Christ in the utmost
extent of its significance.

In Him the whole fullness of the Deity
dwells. This word expresses *permanence,* in
opposition to transitoriness (see Septuagint
version of Genesis xxxvii. 1). The later Gnostics maintained only a transient connection of
the "fullness" with Jesus, and probably the
Colossian heretics had already begun to intimate the same idea. But St. Paul says, it
dwelt in Him. It was not transitory, it was *at*

home.   Thenceforth Jesus has continued to be
the God-man, and shall be forever and forever
(Matt. xxv. 31; Acts xvii. 31).

2. *God was pleased by Him to reconcile all
the things to Himself, having made peace
through the Blood of His cross.*

God was pleased to do this, as having been
pleased that in the Man Jesus the whole fullness of the Godhead should dwell.   On this
fact the work of reconciliation depended, and
it became a fact for the very purpose of that
work being done.   It is a wonderful setting
forth of the importance and glory of the Reconciliation.

A work of reconciliation presupposes opposition, enmity, a derangement of affairs, and is
the bringing about of submission, peace, harmony.   The reconciliation here spoken of is
that *of things to God.*   What things?   *Not* all
things, but "all *the* things"; or, to give the
exact order in the Greek, "*the* all things."   That
is, the all of such things as are *appointed* for
reconciliation.   The definite article here limits
and defines the word "all."   In Philippians iii.
8, Paul says, "I count all things but loss for the
excellency of the knowledge of Jesus Christ,
my Lord," where the article is not inserted before "all things"; but he does insert it in
the words which immediately follow, "for

whom I have suffered the loss of *the* all things"; that is, the all things which he had to lose. He could *count* as loss all things absolutely, but he could not *lose* all things absolutely, since he had not them to lose; hence the article as limiting and defining his actual loss. In Colossians i. 16, 17, we translated the same phrase, "the all things," by *the universe,* as the connection required; but even there the literal force is, In Christ were created *the* all things that were created; precisely according as it is expressed in John i. 3. It is God's good pleasure to reconcile by Christ *the* all things which He has appointed for that purpose, "whether the things on the earth, whether the things in the heavens."

Who and What are Reconciled?

In that purpose of God are *not* included the finally impenitent; for "these shall go away into *everlasting* punishment," precisely as "the righteous into life *everlasting*" (Matt. xxv. 46). Nor the fallen angels; for the Lord Jesus "took not hold of angels, but He took hold of the seed of Abraham" (Heb. ii. 16, 17).

But, in the purpose of God *are* included all men who *become believers in Christ* (Mark xvi. 16). All such are delivered from condemnation, are justified by faith, have peace with God through Jesus Christ, and rejoice in hope of the glory of God (Rom. v. 1, 2; viii. 1).

Creation, also, both animate and inanimate, at least to a certain extent, is included. For, "the earnest expectation of the creation waiteth for the manifestation of the sons of God," and "itself also shall be delivered from the bondage of corruption into the glorious liberty of the children of God." Its various disorders, its "groanings," shall be done away, and God's glory be perfectly reflected in the developed harmony of its many parts. Even "the wolf shall dwell with the lamb, and the leopard shall lie down with the kid; and the calf, and the young lion, and the fatling together; and a little child shall lead them" (Rom. viii. 19-22; Isa. xi. 6-9). Here we see that special relation to creation into which Christ has entered by virtue of His relation to the Church.

And even heavenly things are included. They themselves are purified by the sacrifice of Christ (Heb. ix. 23). That is to say, the blood of Christ reconciles the purity of heaven to the introduction there of such sinners as we have been; purifies the very purity of heaven from the slightest suspicion of complicity with our sin. As Aaron, on the day of atonement, carried blood into the Holy of holies, and put it not alone on the mercy seat, but also on the

floor of the Divine Presence, so "by His own
blood Christ entered" into heaven (Heb. ix.
12), and secured not alone the sinner's person
in reconciliation with God, but also the harmony of heaven's holiness with the redeemed
sinner himself. In this sense the holy angels
themselves are reconciled to God through the
blood of the cross; for while they have no sin
to be atoned for, and need not an expiation for
their own persons, yet, except for the Son of
God's expiatory sufferings for us, their sense
of the sacredness of truth and justice would be
shockingly violated by our appearance as wel-
come dwellers in the august Presence of God.
Not only have they been instructed, and therein
benefited by the work of Christ (Eph. iii. 10),
but also thereby they have been brought into
one mind with God, and are in sweet reconciliation with Him, as regards the salvation of
us sinners; and now there is joy in the presence
of the angels of God over one sinner that re-
penteth (Luke xv. 10). This is another instance of that special relation to creation which
has supervened upon Christ's relation to the
Church.

The Power of the Blood.

Now, while all these reconciliations are effected by God, by means of Christ, yet is it
only as peace is made between God and the

sinner *through the blood of Christ.* Incarnation is not enough; the indwelling of the whole
fullness of the Godhead in the man Jesus, even
as combined with His wondrous teachings,
could not suffice. There must be blood. He
must pass through sufferings and death; and
this, be it noted, not because wicked men would
interrupt Him in His benevolent career, but
because of its being distinctly in the plan of
God that by His sufferings and death He
should accomplish the work of reconciliation.
God *was pleased* to do it by Christ *in this way.*
According to the structure of our text, the
blood of the cross was as much required of
God in order to the reconciling of the things to
Himself and the sinner, as was the indwelling
of the whole fullness of the Godhead in Christ.
The shedding of His blood was the very com-
plement of His Incarnation, for, by the structure of the text, the reconciling could be done
only as the making of peace should be secured;
and peace was made, not through the Incarnation, but through the blood of the cross. Moreover, the verb "to reconcile" and the participle
"having made peace" are both in the aorist
tense, and they both express the fact that the
act of making peace and reconciling was done
at a definite moment, once for all. But that
act, therefore, could not have referred to the

dissolving of the sinner's enmity to God, for
this needs to be done in each successive instance of a sinner's submission to God all along
the ages. The act of making peace must have
referred to the reconciling of God Himself; to
the making it consistent with His Holiness and
Justice to forgive and save the sinner. *That*
having been done, the pure mercy of God
would then have before it an open way for
using the proper means to break down the
enmity of the sinner's ungodliness. God did
require the blood of Him in whom dwelt the
whole fullness of the Godhead; and He would
have died if wicked men had never laid their
violent hands upon Him (Matt. xxvi, 38;
Luke xxii. 44; Isa. liii. 10). God laid upon
Him our iniquities (Isa. liii. 6). He bore our
sins in His own body (1 Pet. ii. 24). His
blood was shed for the remission of our sins
(Matt. xxvi. 28). He who knew no sin was
made sin for us, that we might be made the
righteousness of God in Him (II. Cor. v. 21).
It was *punishment,* then, which Christ suffered; punishment at the hands of God. It was
expiation on our behalf. As well the holiness
and justice of God needed to be reconciled to
the forgiveness of the sinner, as that the sinner's opposition to God needs to be overcome.
And God's own sovereign good pleasure has

provided for both. In purest mercy He gave His eternal Son to bear the curse for us, and thereupon, in purest mercy, He sends to the individual sinner the Holy Spirit, who quickens him into new life, and fills him with loving appreciations of the deliverance effected for him in Christ.

Such are the grounds of Christ's Headship of His Church. In Him dwelt the whole fullness of the Deity, and by Him reconciliation was effected, peace having been made through the blood of His cross. So is He the source of the new creation, and so is He one with His living body, the Church. Let us not forget that His work of reconciliation is a thing in the past, once for all completely accomplished, and is now forever secure. It requires but our faith in Him, that the peace which He perfected shall terminate upon ourselves, and that God's loving presence shall fill our conscious spirits.

11

RECONCILIATION THROUGH THE DEATH OF CHRIST

"And you, that were once alienated, and enemies in your mind, in wicked works, yet now He reconciled in the body of His flesh through death, to present you holy, and without blemish, and uncharged in the presence of Himself" (Col. i. 21, 22).

GOD is the subject of the sentence. It is God who reconciled them, to present them holy, etc., in the presence of Himself; but He did it in the body of *Christ's* flesh through death.

The announcement of His subject-matter being finished, the apostle now proceeds to apply it, and more fully to explain it. Having stated reconciliation by Christ in general terms (v. 20), he here speaks of it in special connection with the Colossian believers, referring to it as a blessing.

1. *What* they were whom God reconciled. They *were once alienated, and enemies in their mind, in wicked works.*

Once they were such: all their lifetime before being reconciled to God. The whole of an unreconciled condition, be it of however long duration, the apostle condenses into a single point of time as regards expression of character. Whatever may be the mental and moral changes of a man through progressive time, whatever his culture in successive years, or whatever his circumstances, his essential character all along, so long as he has not been reconciled to God, is the same as if he had had no progress in time, and his entire duration had been but for an instant. Of every part of his life it must be said, "he is alienated, and an enemy in his mind, in wicked works." He was so *once,* and to that *once* there has never been an interruption. It is once, and the once is always. How very deep are the elements of real character before God! How independent of the surface changes of mere civilization! And what a wonderfully great change is that of reconciliation to God!

Previously thereto a man is *alienated,* estranged from God, and now a stranger to God. This implies that, in his human nature, he has *fallen away* from God; he has become an alien by being *alienated.* (Eccles. vii. 29; Rom. v. 12.) Of necessity, a condition of sin and guilt is one of moral separation from God, of opposition to the holiness and justice of God, of a want of sympathy with Him, and

therefore of ignorance of Him.   Accordingly,
a condition of essential wretchedness; although
the sinner himself may sometimes be oblivious
of it, even as an insane mind is unconscious of
its insanity.   This alienation from God is true
not only of such as were the *heathen* Colossians, not only of the most degraded in human
society, but also of us all, so long as we have
not been brought into one mind with God.
Even Paul said of himself, that he was by nature a child of wrath even as others (Eph.
ii. 3).

And all such are *enemies* to God; not merely
alienated, but hostile. This is an advance on
estrangement. Enemies *in their mind;* in bitter conflict with the will of God, not alone in
the appetites and lower desires of their nature,
but in their very modes of thinking and feeling.   There is often, indeed, in the unreconciled, a conflict of reason and conscience with
the sensual appetites; and yet in that conflict
there is no element of sympathy with the will,
and truth, and ways of God; it is by no means
the same as the conflict of *grace* with nature.
Civilization and culture may do a great deal
for the decencies and proprieties of behavior,
by reason of the temporal well-being depending
upon them; but all the while there may rankle
in the mind a fierce antagonism, no less fierce

because quiet, to God's thinking and teaching. The inner force and the intention of the mind are profoundly *condemnatory* of God Himself, as He is Self-expressed in the word of His truth. The hostility to Him pervades the thoughts and feelings, is *all through the mind* (according to the meaning of the apostle's word here—*dianoia*). The whole history of the human mind is proof of this; *selfism* in thought and purpose has ever been its reigning characteristic; "our lips are our own," say they; "who is Lord over us?" (Ps. xii. 4; see also Rom. viii. 7.)

Now, this alienation and this enmity show themselves *in wicked works.* They must have an expression of themselves, their own sphere of activity. Such a state of mind must work itself out into the deeds of life, the inner deeds and the outer deeds, deeds of the will and deeds of the body. And is not the human mind, enemy to God as it is, well nigh surfeited with wicked works? The noise of them fills the air and stuns the sense of hearing. But even under the fairest exterior of social culture, men "glorify God not as God," and "worship and serve the creature more than the Creator." In their wills and their ways evermore they are transgressing the commandments of God. At home and abroad, in business and in pleasure, they are utterly without any positive submission to, and harmony with, His teachings and requirements; and that being so, even their best things are but transgressions, and, as well in them as in the less cultured portions of society, the alienation and the enmity of their mind are being self-evidenced in the abounding of wicked works. Indeed, by the use of the phrase "their *mind,*" instead of "their *minds,*" the apostle indicates the fact that, in this regard, the mind in one person is one and the same with that in any other person; that all mankind are involved in an organism of sin-ruined humanity; and that if one man needs to be reconciled to God, so likewise every man.

Thus, at the moment that God proceeds to reconcile a man to Himself, that man is under His condemnation. Both legally and judicially the wrath of God abideth on him (Rom. i. 18). And yet it is God Himself who reconciles sinners to Himself; it is not they who do it. He sent His Son into the world "that the world, through Him, might be saved;" and now He is pleased to apply the Saviour's work to that effect. He, the All-righteous, and the offended One, originated the process of reconciliation, and Himself administers it. What utter unworthiness of ourselves on the one hand, what sovereign grace and mercy on the other! "We love Him because He first loved us."

2. God's act of reconciling the Colossians. What was it? How did He proceed? He did it *"in the body of Christ's flesh through death."*

The body of His flesh. Why this double expression? It may have been used in a foresight of the errors of those ancient heretics, the Docetæ, a sect of Gnostics who taught that the Lord Jesus acted and suffered only in appearance; that He had not a real material body. On the contrary, declares the apostle, His body was one of *flesh.* He really suffered and He really died. It may also have been used as distinguishing the body meant from the Church, which had just been spoken of as His body (v. 18). The Gnostic heretic, Marcion, in the second century, finding this word "flesh" to be an insuperable bar against his doctrine of the merely phantom character of the body of Jesus, rejected it from the text here, in defiance of all authority, and then interpreted the word "body" to mean the Church. We thus see of what importance is this double phraseology. It identifies the human body of Christ as being that which is referred to, and it fixes attention on His human capacity for suffering as the sphere in which His work of reconciliation was wrought out. (Compare Eph. ii. 15, 16, where these two words occur again, but separately, and as referring the one to the humanity of Christ, the other to the Church.)*

It is not alone the real, solid humanity of Christ which is here presented to view, but also that humanity as actually suffering. "The body of His flesh *through death.*" This latter circumstance, by the very arrangement of the words, is as essential a part of the process of reconciliation, as is the existence at all of the body of His flesh. His humanity would have been of no avail, except as in His humanity He had actually suffered and actually died. Now this could be only because of His sufferings and death being penal and expiatory. Those for whose reconciling to God He received a body of flesh and died therein were alienated from God and enemies to Him, and were therefore under His sentence of condemnation. But God's condemnation of them must first be done away before any reconcilement to Him could possibly have place. Indeed, it is asserted in our text that the very force of the reconcilia-

---

*[It is hoped the reader will see the application of this to the heresy of Christian Science, which is a form of Gnosticism under another name. It too, denies that Jesus suffered in a real body, and maintains that He only accommodated Himself to our crude notions when He described His body as "flesh and bones." Hence He never truly suffered on the cross and there is no redemption in His blood.—Ed.]

tion effected was, that God presented the condemned ones *"uncharged"* in the presence of
Himself. If they became *uncharged,* of course
the *condemnation* was done away. Since, then,
Christ was appointed to die in order to reconciliation being effected, it follows that He was
appointed to die in order to exempt us from
the penal consequences of our condemnation.
His death was the means of our deliverance
from punishment. But how? What is the
bond of connection between His death and our
deliverance from the condemnation? Did He
Himself, in our stead, suffer under that sentence of condemnation which lay against us,
and in such substitution of Himself for us accomplish our freedom? Beyond question this
is the connecting link.

We are sometimes told, however, that the
sufferings of Christ were meant to be merely
an *illustration* of God's governmental holiness;
that, although those sufferings were not at all
in satisfaction of the sentence of our condemnation, yet the fact that God would not
forgive the sinner without certain great sufferings of Christ, no matter how gratuitous they
were, does imply His jealous regard for the
law which we have violated, and is suggestive
to us that He is determined to uphold its
majesty and truth notwithstanding His inter-

ruption of the penalty in our case. But if the
sufferings of Christ were not the penal consequences of our condemnation, then, in spite of
them, God's exemption of us from the penalty
of the law is His ignoring of the law so far as
we are concerned; and so far from those sufferings illustrating God's jealous determina-
tion to uphold the judicial honor of His government, they really illustrate just the contrary. Such a theory of Christ's sufferings
grounds the sinner's reconciliation to God upon
a principle wholly fictitious. While it describes
God as meaning to make the impression upon
us that thus the law is magnified in the salvation of the sinner, yet, as matter of fact, according to it, God really *demits* the law from
His judicial regards.

Moreover, it leaves out of the account the
penal significance of death itself. In itself
considered, death is punishment; the very punishment threatened and enforced against sinners (Gen. ii. 17; Rom. v. 12). The fact, then,
that He *died,* was the self-assertion of His
bearing punishment; at the same time, the fact
that it was He, the Eternal Son of God in sinless human nature clothed, who died, is the
self-assertion of His bearing punishment not
for Himself, but as the substitute for sinners.
Accordingly, He died not merely the death of

the body, but He endured, for a time, those immeasurable horrors of the Father's *desertion* of Him (Matt. xxvii. 46), which were of a piece with that separation of the soul from God which is the essence of the death pronounced against sinners (II. Thess. i. 9).

Therefore, He did suffer the sinner's punishment. This is the bond of connection between His death and our deliverance from the punishment. He bore the penalty which was our desert, and thereby made us free from the bearing of it. He Himself satisfied the sentence of our condemnation in His substitutionary sufferings, and magnified the law, and made it honorable in the very salvation of such as we.

12

THE RESULTS OF RECONCILIATION

"To present you holy, and without blemish, and uncharged in the presence of Himself" (Col. i. 22).

IN our last lecture we dwelt upon the sinner's reconciliation to God through the death of Christ; in this, continuing our meditation upon the same verses, but especially the latter half of the 22d verse, we wish to speak of the results of that reconciliation on the sinner's side. Let it be noted in passing, however, that it is only one side of the reconciliation which is spoken of in these verses, i.e., the Divine side. In its full sense reconciliation is mutual. That of the sinner to God is one thing; that of God to the sinner is another thing. The former is the subjugation of the sinner's enmity, and his felt submission to God; the latter is God's remission of His sentence of condemnation against the sinner. It is only the latter, God's reconciliation to the sinner, which is here specified. True, the apostle does not use the words, "God's reconciliation to the sinner," but instead, "the sinner's reconciliation to God." But

that by this latter mode of speech he means to
express what in our English idiom would be
stated as God's reconciliation to the sinner, is
evident.   This way of expressing it is according to both the Hebrew and the Hellenistic
idioms.   In I Sam. xxix. 4, it is not said,
"Wherewith shall David reconcile his Master
to himself," but "Wherewith shall he reconcile
himself to his Master"; although it was the
Master's displeasure which was to be removed,
not his own enmity.   In Matthew v. 23, 24, we
are to be reconciled to our brother; and yet the
case supposed is not that of our having a complaint against our brother, but of our brother
having a complaint against us; so that our being reconciled to him is his being conciliated or
appeased toward us.   In II Corinthians v. 19,
it is said, "God was in Christ *reconciling the
world to Himself, not imputing their trespasses to them,"* where it is positively declared
that God's reconciling sinners to Himself consists not in His removing their enmity against
Him, but in removing from them His merited
wrath; "not imputing their trespasses to them."
According to Scripture usage, to reconcile is to
remove the opposition, not from the *offending,*
but from the *offended,* party.   In every instance of the occurrence of this word in the
New Testament, I believe, without exception,

such is its reference; even in our text, although from a misunderstanding of the closing words of it (to be presently explained), it has been thought by many to be an instance to the contrary. Our whole exposition thus far has shown this meaning to be inevitably implied in the apostle's statement of the reconciliation. The sinner's enmity, indeed, is here mentioned, but it is the guilt of that enmity as shutting off God from being at peace with the sinner which is referred to, not the subjective power of it in the sinner's soul. As reconciling the sinner to Himself, God takes away His condemnation from him, thus placing him in a condition of non-controversy toward His justice; so that really, in placing the sinner in an uncharged condition, it is Himself being reconciled to the sinner. This is how we would express it in our English idiom, and this is the side of reconciliation here spoken of; the removal, not of any personal vindictiveness of God, but of His judicial condemnation.

When in His own good time God sends the Holy Spirit to a man, causing him to understand and appreciate the fact that the act of God's reconciliation to him took place completely and finally on the cross of Christ, then is the sinner's enmity broken down, and his own reconciliation to God is effected. Then he believes in Christ, and thereupon the **fact** of his freedom from condemnation is for the first time made known to him. Justification, which is the *pronouncing* righteous, is then pronounced *to him,* and he is able to say, "Therefore, being justified by faith, I have peace with God, through our Lord Jesus Christ." It is God Himself who in this way breaks down the enmity of the sinner; but He does so only because of His merited wrath having been first, and once, and forever, removed from the sinner by Christ in His death.

These two things, that God's reconciliation toward all those for whom Christ died took place *in* and *at* His death, and that it was *complete* and *final,* are the leading features of His procedure in this matter. "Now" He reconciled you, says the apostle. Until Christ had come and borne His people's punishment, there never had been a real reconciliation of God, never an actual *remission* of the condemnation, but only a *passing over* (Rom. iii. 25; Margin) of sins in the prospect of His coming; but now, actually, really, as regards all His people, whether before or since He came, God reconciled you. It is the "now" of complete accomplishment.

But what is this accomplishment? What is that which has thus been wrought out for the sinner as the result of the reconciliation through Christ? This was done so far as the sinner is concerned, *"to present him holy, and without blemish, and uncharged in the presence of Himself."*

1. To present him *holy* in the presence of Himself. This is the word so commonly translated *saints.* Now, in the Acts, the Epistles, and the Apocalypse, all believers in Christ are denominated saints, no matter how great or how small their practical attainments in Christian living. Simply as being in Christ, without reference at all to what may be or may not be their faithfulness of life, they are saints, or holy. This word, then, does not refer in our text to *conduct,* to what is called practical sanctification, but to personal condition before God. The sinner for whom Christ died is invested, to the eye of God, with all the sacredness and the value of His substitutionary sufferings, and with all the righteousness of which those sufferings were the expression. Reconciled to God in those sufferings by having been delivered from the condemnation, he is now also endeared to God by having been completely identified with the excellencies of the righteous Sufferer. And now God has set him in His own very presence as holy, as His own peculiar treasure, as one with Christ in His

regards forever. Such is the instant and invariable effect of God's reconciliation with a sinner.

2. And to present him *without blemish* in *the presence of Himself*. To understand this is of the utmost importance; for thus the word itself demonstrates that the apostle is not here referring to conduct. Of what Christian's practical life could it ever be said, that he is without blemish? To say nothing of his conscious failures, what infirmities belong to him, what unconscious defects, what sins of ignorance. There has never been more than one life in this world which was without blemish. Now it is the identification with that peerless One, whose spotless excellencies enveloped His death for sinners in the sweet incense of perfect satisfaction to Divine Justice, that gives to the sinner for whom Christ died the condition of being without blemish in the Judicial presence of God. We were "made the righteousness of God in Him" (II. Cor. v. 21), and "as He is, so are we in this world" (I. John iv. 17). Perfect in the perfection of Christ! This is the standing, even in the presence of the Infinite and Almighty, given to every sinner with whom He was reconciled in the death of Christ; and every sinner who believes on Christ is thereby assured that God was reconciled with him then.

3. And to present him *uncharged* in the presence of Himself. This word is self-pronounced as a term of personal condition. It does not at all express conduct. It is the very expression of judicial standing. It is that condition of non-liability to punishment which is accorded in Christ to every sinner with whom God became reconciled in the death of Christ. Justice has no indictment to lay upon him, no accusation to bring against him, seeing that justice was fulfilled as regards him in the penal sufferings of his Divinely constituted Substitute. He then became *uncharged;* and he has continued so to be, else it would follow that there were some of his sins to which the sufferings of Christ did not refer. It is that condition of full and final deliverance from the liability to punishment, out of whose felt freedom and love flow all the qualities of genuine obedience, of acceptable conduct before God. He is UNCHARGED: unarraigned, unaccused, pardoned, delivered, set free.

In this exhibition of the fullness of the sinner's changed condition, the apostle pursues the reverse order of statement. Beginning at the highest point (holy), he goes down, through the middle term (without blemish), to the bottom blessing of all (uncharged). It is a descending series, an anti-climax. Here are

three words of personal condition, three great
words of judicial blessing; and although they
make up together a grand structure of blessedness, whose several stories, as it were, are piled
the one upon the other, yet is it all an undi-
vided and indivisible whole of blessing.

God became reconciled to a sinner in the
body of Christ's flesh through death. Instantly
He set that sinner, *uncharged*, in the presence
of Himself. Even God now charged him with
nothing at all. In the searching light of Omni-
science he is not so much as accused. To say
that God does not accuse him, is not only to
say that He does not condemn him, but it is to
say so in the most emphatic and absolute way.
It is the same as saying that God will *remember* his sins no more (Jer. xxxi. 34); that *as
far as the east is from the west,* so far hath He
removed his transgressions from him (Ps. ciii.
12); that He cast all his sins *into the depth of
the sea* (Micah viii. 19). It is a clean sweep
of condemnation from off the entire field of
view.

Such is the perfected condition of every believer in Christ. He has, indeed, his daily
failures and sins, which must needs be confessed and put away; but his confessions are
as those of a child at the feet of his father, and
the Father's forgiveness in the death of Christ

washes off those daily sins, and thus he is kept clean every whit (John xiii. 10). He never becomes an accused culprit at the bar of Justice. His appreciative sense of the Father's love of him will ever prompt him to be sensitive to sin, and cause him to purify his daily conduct; or, if his appreciations grow faint and feeble, and thereby he be betrayed into more or less carelessness of living, then will the Father deal with him according to a father's discipline, but he remains *uncharged*. God is no longer his judge, having already judged him in Christ. He is accused of nothing and never again condemned. His daily failures are dealt with in the intercourse of Father and Son. Perfect in the perfectness of Christ, the Father sees him as without blemish, and feels for him the very endearment with which He looks upon His Only Begotten and Well Beloved. Uncharged of every claim, all his life long, is he who is in Christ.

13

THE EVIDENCE OF RECONCILIATION

"If, indeed ye continue in the faith, having been grounded and settled, and not being moved away from the hope of the Gospel, which ye heard, which was preached in all creation which is under the heaven, whereof I Paul became a minister" (i. 23).

THE great interest in these words is in their connection with what goes before. In the two preceding verses the positive blessing of reconciliation with God is absolutely declared to have been conferred upon these Colossians. "You," says the apostle, "God reconciled in the body of Christ's flesh through death, to present you holy, and without blemish, and uncharged, in the presence of Himself." They *had been* reconciled to God, and therein they *were* presented in His presence as pardoned, and justified, and made sacred to Himself. It was all done. But he adds, "*If indeed,* ye continue in the faith;" or, *Seeing that* ye continue in the faith. *It being a fact* that ye continue in the faith, *therefore* God did pardon and accept you in the body of Christ's flesh, through death. Such is the connection. Your continuing in the faith is proof, at any given moment, that God did; in His purpose, deliver you from your sins, and pronounce you righteous, *in,* and at the time of, the death of Christ. Your present believing on Christ is the one certain premise, and therefrom the conclusion is equally certain, that for you personally Christ was substituted in His sufferings, that your debt of punishment, to the Divine Justice, was then discharged by Him, that from that moment you have been, in God's purpose, uncharged, and without blemish, and holy to Him. God was reconciled to you in the body of Christ's flesh, through death, *seeing that* you are now in the faith. This is the great teaching of our text, and evidently it is of the deepest practical concernment.

1. Let us dwell for awhile on this teaching, and endeavor to develop its riches of meaning.

I am aware that, to many readers of the Bible, the word "If" in the text seems to surround with limitation and uncertainty that declaration of salvation contained in the preceding verses. As if it read, you were saved in the death of Christ, *by reason of* your being now faithful. But the declaration of the preceding verses is absolute: God *did reconcile you* in the death of Christ, to present you uncharged in the presence of Himself. Christ was either a real substitute, bearing the punishment of those for whom He stood, or He was not. If real, then the punishment borne by Him can never be exacted of those for whom He bore it, and their deliverance is an accomplished fact. The deliverance from condemnation which was absolutely accomplished in Christ cannot depend, for its existence, on anything subsequent to His sufferings. It cannot be true that we *were* saved in the death of Christ by reason of our being *now* faithful. It were an absurdity to make the occurrence of what has already taken place to depend on the occurrence of something else in the future. Nor does the apostle's "If" at all countenance such an absurdity, for, as we have seen, his expression is, "If indeed"; *it being so, seeing that.* He is referring to their being in the faith as a present fact, and, as such, *proving* that they *were* saved in, and at the time of, the sufferings of Christ. It being so that ye are in the faith, therefore it is certain that, in the death of Christ, God did present you uncharged in His presence. There is no uncertainty to the believer about his pardon and ac-

ceptance. It was long ago an accomplished
event, and his present faith is to him the demonstration of it.

Again, it has seemed to some as though our
text were teaching this, you *shall get to heaven*
if you continue in the faith. The apostle, however, does not refer here to the getting to
heaven; instead, he is speaking alone of the
believer's personal standing in Christ. *Uncharged and without blemish*. A personal
standing which was effected for the believer at
the time of, and in, the death of Christ, and of
which his present faith is the proof. Certainly,
whoever is uncharged and without blemish in
Christ is already meet for heaven (Col. i. 12);
at the same time it is to that past reconciliation
of God to the believer that reference is here
made, not to the future getting to heaven; and
so the continuing in the faith is here spoken of
as the proof of what is past, not as the condition of what is future. The incorrect translation of the 22d verse in our English version
("unblamable and unreprovable") has fostered
this misconception by creating the impression
that practical conduct is what the apostle is
enforcing. On the contrary, he is teaching
that personal standing of the believer ("without blemish and uncharged"), which is already
a finished achievement.

And, again, our text has been understood by some to imply the doctrine, that the believer may so far lose his faith as to backslide from his personal standing in Christ, and be finally lost. "If ye continue in the faith," they regard as equivalent to "ye may lose your faith, and therein also your condition of deliverance from condemnation." But such is by no means the construction of the text, and, whether this doctrine be true or false, it is demonstrably not the teaching here. The text does not say, that something *shall be,* if something else *shall be;* but, that something *was,* if something else *is.* It speaks of a present faith as the proof of a past fact. Ye *were* delivered from condemnation and accepted of God, *seeing that ye are now* in the faith. No reference is here made to the future, no doubt of any kind is insinuated, no threatening of danger is implied. The apostle's purpose is simply to state the absolute accomplishment of salvation in the past sufferings of Christ, and the demonstration of it which is furnished to an individual soul in the present existence of his faith.

And now, in this clear understanding of the text, we are enabled to see how precious it is. The believer's deliverance and acceptance are finished facts of the past, and the link *consciously* connecting him therewith is simply

that he is a believer. He did become uncharged, and without blemish, and holy to God,
when and in that Christ died, and he knows
that he did, just for the reason that he is now
trusting and resting in Christ's death.

For faith is the gift of the Holy Ghost
(Rom. xiii. 3; Phil. i. 29). The moral ability
to appreciate, and consent to, and realize my
ruined estate by nature, and thereupon to appreciate, and consent to, and appropriate the
sufferings of Christ, as having exhausted in
His person my own indebtedness of punishment, all which is simply faith, comes only
from the in-working of the Spirit of God
(Rom. viii. 7). When, therefore, He does
cause me to understand both myself and the
work of Christ, and to appropriate it, it is the
same as His telling me that I was identified
with Christ in all His sufferings, that He did
discharge in full my own particular debt, and
that, as matter of fact, I was then, in the purpose of God, presented in His presence as absolutely uncharged. I know of God's past and
finished reconciliation to me by my present
reconciliation to Him; for faith is the heart's
submission to God.

The apostle having spoken in the two preceding verses of God's reconciliation to us, he
speaks in this verse of our reconciliation to

Him. That was finished on the cross; this is effected by the Holy Ghost working in us, faith in Christ. Thus in those verses and in this, as taken together, the subject of Reconciliation is presented on both its sides. The believer was judicially delivered, and now he is consciously so.

It is of the very significance of the text, then, to teach us that we may be evermore rejoicing in an assurance of our perfected salvation in Christ. If we are conscious of the faith, then do we know that the heart of God was set upon us, ages ago, in the sufferings of Christ, and that then and there we were actually set down in the presence of Him whose existence is eternal, as uncharged, and without blemish, and holy to Him? But if we are not conscious of the faith, we can have no such assurance. No one who is without this understanding of himself as a sinner, and of Christ as his substitute, and this reception of it all, has any evidence that he was personally considered of God in the sufferings of Christ, and that it was his particular debt which Christ then discharged.

Thus there is a warning in the text; a call to self-examination. *Are* we in the faith? See to it. Be clear and distinct in your convictions.

II. What is that condition of mind here called a continuance in the faith? "Seeing that ye continue in the faith, *having been grounded and settled, and not being moved away from the hope of the Gospel.*"

(1) It is such confidence as is sustained by clear and strong convictions of the truth. The Colossians were continuing in the faith, *having been grounded.* They had been built up from deep-dug foundations. Notice the expression *"the* faith." That is, the faith which is taught in the Gospel; the principles, the doctrines, the truths, which constitute the Gospel. In these they had been grounded. Man's estate as a sinner, as alienated from God and an enemy to Him, as condemned, as utterly unable to procure a righteousness for himself; the work of Christ, who, the Sinless, was yet the Sin-bearer, having been made sin for us, that we might be made the righteousness of God in Him; the believer's finished deliverance in Christ, and his perfected justification in the presence of God; on such subjects they had been definitely instructed, their perceptions were clear, and their consent was cordial. Hence the false teachers at Colossæ had made, as yet, but little progress. Such convictions are the very strength of personal trust in Christ. And they are the living principle of

personal victory over the world. In their own
effulgent light of blessedness they obscure
alike the false glory of all godless speculations
and the pleasures of sin for a season. They
adapt the soul to the service of God, as fire
conforms the liquid metal to a prepared mould.
In such convictions of "the faith" there is ever
the exercise of faith. True, such an one may
suffer his convictions to get dim, and then his
personal trust will get cold; but he is sure,
sooner or later, to get back its warmth, for
when convictions on these subjects, and so
clear and strong, have once pervaded the soul
and gone down to the roots of conscious moral
life, no other thoughts can ever bring satisfaction. The intensity of his consciousness may
occasionally subside, but he is neither a "stony-
ground hearer" nor a "thorny-ground hearer"
(Matt. xiii. 20-22). He came to the exercise
of faith by having been grounded in the faith,
and a true believer he continues to be. He
had been *grounded;* established as on a foundation. Thence he has become *settled;* fixed
as in a seat thereon. And now he *continues;*
resting in the seat, remaining on the foundation.

(2) A continuance in the faith is the not
"being moved away from the hope of the Gospel." This is the negative side of the continu-

ance. We may ask ourselves, are we continuing in the faith? Or else, are we being moved away from the hope of the Gospel? It is the same subject from different points of view. If the hope of the Gospel is being maintained within us, we are certainly continuing in the faith; and if we are continuing in the faith, the hope of the Gospel is certainly being maintained within us. The hope inspired by the Gospel is that joyous anticipation of future glory which is the product of clear and cordial convictions of the truth, especially with regard to the work of Christ as having finished and secured the believer's deliverance and righteousness. Hence, the hope will be enjoyed in the proportion of the convictions, and the convictions must have been clear and cordial in the proportion of the hope. Blessed, indeed, is a continuance in the faith. It is a condition, as fully expressed, of clear and distinct thinking, of cordial consenting, of personal triumphing in the work of Christ, of present enjoying, and of never-disappointed hoping. Is it our state of mind? Why not? It depends only on true and cordial thoughts of Christ. Examine your thoughts of Christ by the old gospel of the Bible. "The gospel which ye *heard,*" said Paul to the Colossians. Not what they were now hearing from certain false teachers; but what they heard from Epaphras in the past, and at the first. Their first hearing was of the genuine gospel; and that same old gospel is now upon the imperishable pages of the New Testament.

14

THE MINISTRY OF RECONCILIATION

"I now rejoice in my sufferings for you, and am filling up the things lacking of the afflictions of Christ in my flesh for His body's sake, which is the Church; whereof I became a minister, according to the stewardship of God, which was given to me for you, to fulfil the word of God" (i. 24, 25)

HAVING referred to the fact of his ministry in the last clause of the 23d verse, and leaving that fact to have its due influence on the Colossians, the apostle now passes to his personal experiences in the ministry. *He was rejoicing in it.* But his ministry had brought upon him many sufferings; nevertheless he rejoiced. Nay, his sufferings were what he endured *for them,* since they came upon him in the execution of his ministry among the Gentiles; and he had joy in suffering for them. *Now* he rejoiced; even with the chain around his wrist. He continued to rejoice, after so many years of his suffering ministry. But what was the source of his joy? The salvation in Christ which was his, and which he trusted his ministry, through Epaphras, had caused to be theirs also (vs. 21, 23). What a glorification of the Gospel which he preached was this, his joy, in such circumstances! What a powerful personal appeal to them, as against those false teachings which would lead them away from the truth as it is in Jesus.

Such is the general connection. But this thought of Gospel joy in the midst of sufferings is carried yet further by the particular expressions of the text. We are told of a glorious truth; of something we need to know and to think of for our support under trials, and for our quickening in interest and zeal. It is a certain relationship in which believers stand, *by reason of their sufferings,* to both Christ and the Church. Our sufferings are *the filling up of the things lacking of the afflictions of Christ,* and they are so *for His body's sake, the Church.*

I. Let us examine what the apostle says of His sufferings. He says three things.

(1) His sufferings were *for* His brethren. On their behalf. To their advantage. This is the truth of our effective influence upon each other. We are mutual helpers, as well by means of our sufferings as in other ways. By our patience and constancy we may lead others into, and confirm them in, the faith of the Gospel, and so be instrumental in their obtaining

the salvation which is in Christ Jesus with eternal glory (2 Tim. ii. 10). By the comforts wherewith God has comforted us in our trials, we are enabled to comfort others when troubled, either in body or mind, and to strengthen and establish them in all Gospel realizations and joys (II. Cor. i. 4). With this aspect of the subject we are generally familiar.

But (2) His sufferings were "the filling up, in his flesh, of the things lacking of the afflictions of Christ." What do these words mean?

It has been understood by many that "the afflictions of Christ," as here intended, is but another name for Paul's afflictions. His afflictions were Christ's, on the principle that the Head does Himself suffer in the sufferings of His members (Acts ix. 4, 5; Matt. xxv. 40, 45; I. Cor. xii. 12; II. Cor. i. 5). Such an interpretation of this phrase is in perfect accord with the usages of Scripture. According to this understanding, the words of the text would mean that Paul was filling up in his afflictions the things lacking of his afflictions. That is to say, he was going on to endure whatever remained of the afflictions which God had appointed for him to endure. Meanwhile he was comforted by the fact that his afflictions were also Christ's. It is indeed a

blessed truth that our afflictions occur to us
only as measured, and numbered, and chosen
for us by our Covenant God, and that beyond
an amount graciously fixed they cannot go
(I. Thess. iii 3; Job v. 6, 17, 18; Jer. xlvi. 28).
And it is a most blessed truth that the Head
and the members are one, that Christ regards
His people as He regards Himself; that their
sufferings are His sufferings.

But the question is, Are these the teachings
of this place? If "the afflictions of Christ" be,
as here used, but another name for those of
His people, then such an understanding of
these words of our text is the true one. If,
however, it should appear that this phrase
must be taken in the sense of the personal
afflictions of Christ, then the whole aspect of
the passage would be changed. Now, the
reigning idea of this 24th verse is, that the
apostle's sufferings were the means of his
rendering service to his Christian brethren.
He does not refer at all to the number of his
appointed sufferings, but only to his being enabled, by means of his sufferings, to do good.
"My sufferings *for* you," he says. And in this
connection it is that he speaks of those sufferings of his as supplying a certain lack in what
he calls "the afflictions of Christ." So that
plainly the lack referred to is one of service—

the service which afflictions are meant to render. And this is further made evident by the statement that the lack here referred to is to be supplied *"for the sake of Christ's body, which is the Church."* What was lacking, then, was not what remained to be endured of his appointed afflictions, but a certain proportion of that service to the Church, which it is the design of afflictions to contribute. Of such service there was a lack in what he calls "the afflictions of Christ," and his own afflictions were intended to supply that lack. If, then, we understand "the afflictions of Christ" as being, in this place, but another name for the apostle's afflictions, what he says is this, "I am filling up in my afflictions what is lacking of service in my afflictions." That is to say, his going on to endure the afflictions yet remaining to him would be to render the portion yet lacking of the service, for the sake of which his afflictions were being sent upon him. Which is merely a bald truism; a puerility that we should not expect to find in any dignified statement. Besides, why, in such a sentence, should the apostle call his afflictions "the afflictions of Christ?" Why should he call up the idea of the Head suffering in the members? If his purpose had been to refer to the comfort possible to him in the endurance of afflictions, or

in the rendering of the service which afflictions
are designed to furnish, then there might have
been a reason for so designating them (II. Cor.
i. 5) ; but when, according to this understanding of the words, he merely stated the fact of
there being in his afflictions a lack of service,
certainly, in that connection, to name his afflictions "the afflictions of Christ" was in no sense
necessary, and would rather seem to be an im-
pertinence. The thought of the Head suffering
in the members had no place in so naked a
statement of the apostle's own lack. Assured-
ly, then, this phrase, "the afflictions of Christ,"
is not used here for the purpose of designating
the apostle's own afflictions. It means the personal afflictions of Christ Himself. And what
St. Paul says is this, that his afflictions supplied
that proportion of service to the Church which
was lacking in the personal afflictions of Christ.

But now how are we to take this? Not as
referring at all to the *expiatory* character of
the sufferings of Christ, of course. The apostle has already said in this chapter that "in
Christ all fullness dwelt" (v. 19) ; that accordingly He "did make peace through the blood
of His cross" (v. 20), having completely
wrought that effect in His own sufferings
alone, and that, by consequence, God had already "reconciled to Himself" the Colossian

believers, "in the body of Christ's flesh, through death," and had presented them *holy, and without blemish, and uncharged,* in the *presence of Himself*" (vs. 21, 22). Perfection of atonement can go no further. Thus, not the shadow of a support from our text has the Roman Catholic doctrine of Indulgences, by which that church claims to be able, by applying the superabounding merits of the saints, to grant remission of the temporal punishment due to sins of others, and to save sinners from purgatory. The saints are utterly without any atoning merits of their own (Eph. ii. 8, 9; Rom. xi. 6); they are ever unprofitable servants (Luke xvii. 10); they have no works of supererogation; they cannot compensate for the sins either of themselves or of others (I. John i. 7). But if we can *contribute* nothing to the atoning sufferings of Christ, yet we can have the *fellowship* of those sufferings, even in their atoning character. By reason of the believer's judicial standing in Him, what He suffered as bearing the punishment of sin the believer also suffered. "I have been crucified with Christ," said Paul (Gal. ii. 20). "Ye died with Christ," he said again (Col. ii. 20). And so, "ye were raised together with Christ" (Col. iii. 1); as He triumphed, precisely so did we triumph. This, however, is but the con-

ferring upon us of all the merits of Christ
Himself; not at all the claiming of any merits
of our own. It is *as if* we had personally done
it all, though we only did it substitutionally;
yet therein we really did it *judicially*. Yes, we
have the fellowship of even the atoning sufferings of Christ; they were endured in our
name, and judicially they are ours. But they
were personally His alone.

In this connection further, notice the word
thlipseis, translated "afflictions" in this case.
Everywhere else is it applied in the New Testament only to the distresses and trials of men,
and here alone to the personal sufferings of
Christ. Never is it applied to Him elsewhere.
A further guarding this on Paul's part, against
being misunderstood as referring to Christ's
expiatory sufferings. He is considering them
now, and for the moment, the same as he
would speak of our afflictions. Never, indeed,
can Christ's sufferings be divested of their
atoning efficacy, but we may contemplate them
now in one way and now in another.

We cannot imitate him in the atonement of
His sufferings, but we can imitate Him as being in afflictions; else, how could we be exhorted to "suffer with Him" (Rom. viii. 17; II.
Tim. ii. 12)? "The sufferings of this present
time" have nothing in common with His suf-

ferings as an Expiatory Passion, but we may suffer with Him as He endured afflictions. The fact of affliction is common to Him and us, although qualities of affliction are different as between Him and us. The head and the body may suffer together, each its own particular pain. In either one it is pain, and so they have a community of suffering. But the pain in the head is of a sensation different from that in the members, and therein they have not a community of suffering. Keeping ever in its unapproachable preëminence the atoning character of the sufferings of Christ, we may then further consider them in the light of afflictions, and, taking our stand in imitation of Him, become co-workers with Him, both as to the conduct we should pursue under our own afflictions, and as to the service which they are intended to render to the Church.

Now, in what way did the afflictions, merely as such, of the Lord Jesus do service to His people? They educated His manhood into sympathy with them, and, for their instruction and strengthening, gave many occasions for the display of the graces of the Spirit in His wonderful life among men. For "He learned obedience by the things which He suffered" (Heb. v. 8), and "in that He Himself hath suffered, being tempted, He is able to succor them

that are tempted" (Heb. ii. 18). He felt the
pangs of hunger; he knew the sensation of
loneliness, and the yearning for sympathy
(Matt. xxvi. 38); He was tortured by bodily
pain, and went down to the depths of mental
anguish; He was exposed to the malice of enemies, and subjected to the powers of darkness
(Luke xxii. 53); He "offered up prayers and
supplications, with strong crying and tears,
unto Him that was able to save Him from
death, and was heard in that He feared" (Heb.
v. 7). So did His life abound in occasions for
the exercise of meekness, and patience, and
gentleness, and for teaching the wholesome
lessons of such graces. So was He prepared
to "have compassion on the ignorant, and on
those that are out of the way" (Heb. v. 2).
So had He "the tongue of the learned, that He
should know how to speak a word in season to
him that is weary" (Isa. l. 4). Such was the
ministry of his afflictions. The atonement
which he was working out, by means of the
inflictions of Divine Justice upon Him as the
Incarnate Son of God, gave rise to His being
in a condition to endure afflictions, and created
the opportunity for this display of character
and sympathy; but over and above the *salvation* resulting to His people from His atoning
passion, was this beneficial service of simply

His afflictions. This is what they did for His
people "in the days of His flesh," and that is
what they are still doing for them because of
their recital in the Word of God. And precisely this is the service in which, in the midst of
our own afflictions, we, His disciples, may and
are bound to follow Him.

Nay, it is His lack of service in this regard
which is required from us. Not that He failed
in any particular therein; He did good absolutely and all-inclusively. But this kind of
service is never finished. Forever there will be
something lacking of it, so long as afflictions
exist in the world, and the beneficial influences
of them shall be an element in God's government of men. The atoning sufferings of
Christ were absolutely finished; endured "once
for all;" neither can they ever be repeated, nor
can any one add thereto. But in this service of
afflictions every child of God is associated with
his Saviour; and never will it be completed as
a grand whole till the last contribution of influence shall have been rendered from the last
existing affliction among the children of God.
Paul was doing his part, by reason of his afflictions, toward the filling up of this lack; and in
the afflictions of every Christian a like part is
ever to be performed.

Thus, the saved in Christ are exalted to be

co-workers with Him in their trials and distresses. He and we are united together in the same grand work. We are even doing the same that He did, for we are filling up the lack in the service of His afflictions. We do not equal Him in either the extent or the effectiveness of the service; but in the reality of it we are one with Him. And since our persons have been pardoned, and made righteous, and made holy to God, in His expiatory blood, and we are even as He is before the Father (I. John iv. 17), so is our service elevated to an equality of acceptance with His (Eph. v. 2; II. Cor. ii. 15).

(3) The sufferings of Paul were a filling up of the lacking service of Christ's afflictions *for His body's sake, which is the Church.* The service of our sufferings is rendered to God's people, not alone as individuals, but also as a body, a great corporation of persons and blessedness. In our Christ-like conduct under suffering, not only are we doing good to this and that one, but we are contributing to the building up and the completion of the Church of God. As matter of fact, the Church is not built up without the reciprocal service of its members; from Christ, the Head, the whole body, fitly joined together and compacted, carries on the increase of itself by means of every

joint of supply, according to energy in the measure of each single part (Eph. iv. 15, 16). On the part of the Church of the saved in heaven, what joys of self-development in Christ there will be, since all will have contributed to their own building up, as well as what perfection of eternal salvation in the blood and righteousness of Christ! What precious things are our afflictions, since even they are exalted into fountains of service toward the realization of that vision of beauty and glory in heaven.

15

THE MYSTERY OF THE GLORY

"The mystery which hath been hid from the ages
and from the generations, but now was made manifest to His saints, to whom God did will to make
known what is the riches of the glory of this mystery
among the Gentiles, which is Christ in you, the hope
of glory" (i. 26, 27).

THE apostle had spoken of his having become a minister "to fulfil the word of
God" (v. 25). To that phraseology he
now gives a special direction, for "mystery" is in apposition with "word of
God." He describes this mystery as
what had always been hidden, and only
recently revealed; as something, therefore,
which till now had not formed a part of the
Word of God. This he had in charge to make
known. So that his "fulfilling" the Word of
God was his completing that Word, supple-
menting it, making it a fuller Word of God
than it had ever been before. It was given to
him to fill out and perfect the Word of God in
this particular. This was the special feature

of that stewardship of God which had been committed to him (v. 25. And compare Eph. iii. 2-9). And what a magnificent addition he had been enabled to make, by revelation, to the teachings of the Old Testament, he proceeds to state in the verses of our text. All this was another item in the apostle's personal appeal to the Colossian believers. It was he to whom this mystery had been revealed, and in whose charge it had been placed. Wherefore, by the greatness of such a revelation, by its authority, its blessedness and glory, they should not give way to the oppositions of science, falsely so called, but should remain firm to the doctrines of his preaching.

Let us consider his definition of the mystery, *which is Christ in you, the hope of the glory."*

At first sight these words might seem to be but a statement of the fact, that those who are Christ's are indeed saved by Him. And yet that which these words express is what had been "hidden from the ages and from the generations," and was only now made manifest. This is that, the riches of whose glory God was pleased to make known just now for the first time; which, by special revelation to himself, Paul had added to the word of God, so "fulfilling," completing, that word. We are sure, therefore, that an analysis of this defini-

tion of the mystery must and will exhibit to us
far more than merely the fact of salvation by
Christ, whether from condemnation, or unto
everlasting life. Salvation by Christ, from sin
and unto eternal life, had been revealed in the
older Scriptures. (See such places as Isa. liii.;
Job xix. 25-27; Isa. xxvi. 19; Daniel xii. 2.)
We are told, indeed, that Christ "brought life
and immortality to light through the Gospel"
(II. Tim. i. 10). Certainly so; but not in the
sense of bringing them into the light for the
first time. Literally, He threw light upon
them (*photisantos*); that is, more light. He
illuminated the truths which had been already
announced; He shone upon them, and made
them brighter and more comforting. On the
contrary, what is said in our text, "Christ in
you, the hope of the glory," is declared here,
as also in the parallel place in the Ephesians
(iii. 2-9), to have beeen hidden from all preceding times, and never to have been announced till revealed to Paul. It must have,
then, a more extended meaning than merely
the being saved by Christ.

Let us refer to that passage in the Ephesians,
which is another definition of the same mystery
by the same apostle. We shall perceive at
once, that, as in our text it is called "this mystery among the Gentiles," so there it is made to

consist in the association of Gentiles with Jews
as regards certain blessings in Christ. But
what blessings? The Old Testament is express that Gentiles, as well as Jews, should be
saved by Christ. Paul himself quotes from it,
for the very purpose of proving his point, testimony after testimony to this effect (Rom.
xv. 9-12). It did declare that Gentiles should
trust in Christ, that He should be the Leader
and High Priest of their worship, that they
should praise Him, and rejoice with the ancient
people. The salvation of Gentiles by Christ
was not that which had been secreted from the
ages and from the generations, and only just
now made known to Paul. What association
in blessing, then, of Gentiles with Jews is
meant? We have an explicit answer in the
Ephesians. "That the Gentiles should be fellow-heirs, and of the same body, and joint partakers (Greek) of the promise in Christ by the
Gospel." *Fellowship,* then, is the principle of
the association in Christ of Jews and Gentiles;
their fellowship together in all spiritual and
heavenly blessings in Christ. This is more
than simply the salvation of Gentiles as well
as Jews; it is salvation with *equal* heirship, and
equal membership in the one body of Christ,
and *equal* participation of the promise in Christ
by the Gospel. And this is the meaning of our

text. "Christ in you," in you *Gentiles,* "the hope of the glory;" *the* glory, glory in its widest sense, including all glory, just as "the promise," in the Ephesian passage, is promise in its widest sense, including all promises, all blessing, all glory. "The hope of the glory" corresponds to "the partaking of the promise." Gentile believers have the hope of the uttermost glory; Jewish believers can have no more. So that our text implies what is expressed in the Ephesian passage, the equal heirship, the equal membership, and the equal partaking of the promise. It is FELLOWSHIP. Gentile believers are *fellows* of the Jewish, in the fullness of the blessing of the Gospel of Christ. This is what had been hid from all previous times, but was now specially revealed to Paul.

1. *Equality of personal standing in Christ* is a part of this fellowship. To be in Christ as equal heirs, and equal members of His one body, and equal partakers of the promise in Him, is, of course, to have an equal standing in acceptance before God. Now it is in the nature of the case, that all who are saved by Christ must be equally acceptable to God. The sinner for whom Christ died has Christ for his Substitute, who bare his sins in His own body, who satisfied God's justice for him, and who finished the satisfaction. Therefore that

sinner's punishment cannot now be exacted of
him. He is one with Christ, and as Christ is,
in His own perfect acceptance before the
Father in His work, so is He. He is presented
before God *uncharged, and without blemish,
and holy to Him.* The personal acceptance of
no one can go beyond this. And so, if the Old
Testament predicted that Gentiles, as well as
Jews, should be saved by Christ, it also implied, in the nature of the case, that the personal standing in Christ of the one would be as
perfect as that of the other. This, however,
was only an implication, it was not asserted
there; nor, without the additional light thrown
upon the subject by the Gospel, could it be
certainly reasoned out from the Scriptures of
the Old Testament. We have the positive declaration of St. Paul, that while the subject-
matter of the new revelation made to him was
indeed implicitly contained in the Scriptures of
the Prophets, yet it had never been detected
there till that revelation was made (Rom. xvi.
25, 26). The all-perfect personal acceptance
in Christ of any saved man, beyond question, is
involved in the 53d chapter of Isaiah and in
other places; but so literally taken must be the
fact of substitution, in order to the Gospel understanding of Christ's work, and so necessary
is express Divine authority for a sinner's ven-

turing to appropriate to himself the very perfection of the work of his great Substitute, no process of mere inference could sufficiently assure the mind. We know how difficult it is for ourselves to become established, even amid our present blaze of Gospel light, in a clear and assured conviction of the truth in this matter. The intelligent, devout Jew might have learned from his Scriptures, that his Messiah would save Gentiles; but he would not have learned from them that all fullness of blessing should be given to others, as well as to his own nation. Hence the importance of the new revelation to Paul. And how magnificently he states it. Dying and rising with Christ, seated with Him in the heavenlies, made the righteousness of God in Him, uncharged, and without blemish, and holy in the presence of God, and blessed with all spiritual blessing in Christ; all this he says of every believer, whether Jew, whether Gentile.

2. Association together of Jews and Gentiles *in the Church of the Glorified* is another part of their fellowship; for they equally have the "hope of the glory," they are "fellow-heirs, and fellow-members of the same body, and fellow-partakers of the promise in Christ by the Gospel." The Church of the glorified is presented to us, in its heavenly condition, in the

4th and 5th chapters of the Revelation, under
the symbols of the Elders and the Living
Creatures. Elsewhere it is called "the Church
of the *first-born ones*" (Heb. xii. 23) ; the first-
born from among the dead; all those who shall
have part in the first resurrection at the second
coming of Christ (1 Cor. xv. 23; Rev. xx. 6) ;
those who, in the words of the Saviour, "shall
be accounted worthy to obtain the resurrection
which is from among the dead" (Luke xx, 35,
the Greek). Immediately after their resurrection, and together with the believers who shall
then be alive, they "shall be caught up in the
clouds, to meet the Lord in the air;" but
thence they shall return with Him to the earth
(I. Thess. iv. 14-17; Zech. xiv. 5; Rev. xix.
14). The heavenly Jerusalem will be their
home (Heb. xi. 10; Rev. xxi. 10, 27), and yet
they shall reign with Christ on the earth (Rev.
v. 10; xx. 6). Thus, nations shall still exist on
the earth, both Jews and Gentiles, and among
them shall be the Church of Jesus Christ
(Zech. xiv. 9, 11; Isa. ii. 2-4; lxii. 1-4; I. Cor.
xv. 25). On the one hand, the risen Church
of the glorified, then reigning on earth; on the
other hand, the Millennial Church of men in
the flesh, and in the midst of an earthly condition. But those two will be but one Church;
the same one body of Christ, in which all saved

ones are one with the Head, even as all
branches are one with the vine. The personal
standing in Christ of believers then in the flesh
will be as perfect as will be the personal standing in Christ of the then glorified; and yet
those will differ from these, as not being, like
them, glorified. Circumstances will respective-
ly vary, and, for the time being, a better kind of
blessedness will be enjoyed by the glorified,
than by those who, while being equally accepted in Christ, will yet not have been glorified.
As, between the two classes, there will be a
certain inequality, a certain lack of fellowship.
Ultimately, since every one in Christ is a joint-
heir with Him (Rom. viii. 17), even that inequality shall be done away, and the Millennial
Church itself be exalted to the estate of the
glorified (Rev. xxi. 1-7). But God is sov-
ereignly gracious, and while presenting all
those whom He reconciled in Christ as equally
uncharged, and without blemish, and holy, in
the presence of Himself, and delighting in
them even as He delighteth in Christ, He may,
as He think best, apportion His bestowments
of blessing differently. No inequality, however, shall have place in the Church of the
glorified, as regards Jews and Gentiles. God
wills it thus. The membership of that Church
is now being prepared; all God's people, from

Adam down to the Second Coming, be they of
Israel or of the Gentiles, are to be the members
of it (Gal. iii. 9, 14, 28, 29) ; and when the pre-
determined number shall have been fulfiled
(Rom. xi. 25), then shall be ministered to
every one of them an equal entrance into the
glory. None of them shall fail of it, nor shall
any one of them precede another; the dead in
Christ out of all the ages, although with Him
and blessed, not as yet having been glorified.
"God having provided some better thing for
us, that they without us should not be made
perfect" (Heb. xi. 40).

3. Of that *fellowship* in glory the Old
Testament said nothing. Intimations of *the
glory* it did give, but they were mentioned only
in connection with Israel (Isa. xxvi. 19; Dan.
xii. 2). It required a new revelation for its
announcement. And Paul did announce it.
"When Christ, your life, shall appear, then
shall ye also appear with Him in glory" (Col.
iii. 4). And so, again and again. Meanwhile,
the other apostles taught the same truth, and
the New Testament teems with its preciousness. It is, indeed, "the promise in Christ by
the Gospel." It *is* the Gospel. It is salvation
in its highest and fullest results. It is the
truth as it is in Jesus. *"Christ in you,* the hope
of the glory," saith our text.

4. Only as Christ is in us is He to us the hope of the glory. Christ in us is a life; it is Himself living in us (Gal. ii. 20). It is our loving God, and having the spirit of obedience to Him (John xiv. 23). It is also a spiritual practical power enabling us to overcome the world (I. John iv. 4). It implies, therefore, a new heart; a born childhood to God. Hence Christ in us is alone that which secures to our experience the hope of the glory. In the corruption of our hearts we indulge false hopes. But when we have new hearts, and are feeling the constraining sweetness of His indwelling, then have we the power, the yearning sympathy with the truth, the self-enforcing life, whereby to lay hold on Himself as the very principle of our hope.

5. Thus, if Christ be in us, we also are *in Him*. For how shall He be present in such guilty souls as we, and not bring us, by very force of His presence, into the condition of resting in Him as the atonement for our sins? The principle underlying the Scriptural phrase, "In Christ," is that we were represented in His expiatory sufferings, and truly so by reason of His having been constituted one with us. Accordingly, His people are said *to have been crucified with Him* (Gal. ii. 20), and it is declared that God became reconciled to them *"in*

the body of Christ's flesh through death" (Col. i. 22). To the eye of God they were in Christ on the Cross. The effect of this upon them has been that their condemnation was taken away (Rom. viii. 1), and they became "uncharged" (Col. i. 22); also that they were presented "without blemish and holy in God's presence" (Col. i. 22), for, as being in Christ Jesus, He was made unto them "righteousness and sanctification" (1 Cor. i. 30). Now, except as having been thus delivered from our sins, how were it possible for Christ to live in us? Could He vouchsafe His abiding presence in a soul condemned to everlasting banishment from God? And if He come into those who were thus represented and expressed in Himself on the cross, must He not move them to recognize this their relation to Him, and to trust in Him in this regard? So that, if we have faith in His atoning merits, it proves our being in Him. Therefore, if Christ be in us, we shall evidence it in the exercises of such faith (2 Cor. xiii. 5; Phil. iii. 9). And so, He being in us, we are sure to seize upon Himself with our hearts as the ground, the substance, and the security of our hope. He being in us, the hope of the glory will as spontaneously leap into action, as the season of Spring.

Have we Christ in us, then? Is it self-expressed in our apprehending that we are in Him? Are we resting only in "the righteousness which is through the faith of Christ?" Or, are we intent on "having our own righteousness," not as yet convinced of our ruin and wretchedness, and only scorning the fear of being "dogged by the hunting hell-hounds of our deservings?" We are in Christ, if Christ be in us; and if He be not in us, then have we not the glory in us. He that now takes Christ shall then take the glory.

16

THE GLORY OF THE MYSTERY

"The riches of the glory of this mystery among the Gentiles, which is Christ in you, the hope of the glory" (i. 27).

IN our last lecture we considered the mystery of the glory, in this let us look at the glory of the mystery. But first to consider the meaning of the word "mystery" a little further.

This word is derived from one (*muo*) which means to shut the lips, and the root of which (*mu*), has been formed into our English word, *mum*. The root idea of mystery is secrecy, concealment. But, forasmuch as the secrets of the so-called mysteries among the Greeks were made known to the initiated, it came to contain within itself, and to connect them together, the two diverse ideas of concealment and disclosure. A mystery was that which could not be known except as revealed, but which was revealed. And according to this is its usage in our text. "The mystery which hath been hidden, but now was made manifest." "This mystery among the Gentiles": divulged among

them (compare Rom. xvi. 25. Especially Eph.
iii. 5). This fulness of the Gospel, especially
as being intended of God for Gentiles as well
as Jews, had been concealed "from the ages,"
the longer periods, and "from the generations,"
the shorter periods which make up an age: that
is to say, from the beginning and all along.
But *now* it *was* made manifest: now in the
apostle's time, the revelation of it being an historical fact. God's own inscrutable secret, yet
now by Him made known.

Properly, then, a mystery. St. Paul borrowed from the Greeks their own word, and, bap-
tizing it into the sublime meaning of the Gospel, thereby covered with contempt the boasted
revelations of heathenism. How transcendent
is this disclosure of the secret of God. This
mystery is really what the wisdom of Greece
did but vainly pretend to be; such knowledge
of hidden things of the Infinite Mind, as gives
us assurance of our blessedness, and is so gracious and so glorious. God "did will" to make
them known; moved thereto out of His own
good pleasure, and in His amazing grace to
sinful men. And, unlike the heathen mysteries,
which were even offered only to the aristocratic
few, this true mystery is offered to all. It is
the mystery among the nations; there being
now no more of reserve than of secrecy. Yea,

"we *speak* the wisdom of God in a mystery, even the hidden wisdom which God ordained before the world unto our glory. Eye hath not seen, nor ear heard, neither have entered into the heart of man, the things which God hath prepared for them that love Him. But God hath revealed them to us by His Spirit; for the Spirit searcheth all things, yea, the deep things of God" (1 Cor. ii. 7).

Now what is the glory of this mystery?

From his definition of the mystery—"Christ in you (Gentiles), the hope of the glory"—it will be seen that the mystery is not the glory hoped for, but the hope of the glory. It is the privilege of their enjoying the hope. When he speaks, then, of "riches of the glory of this mystery," he means the riches of the glory of *hoping for* the glory. This hope, as entertained by Jew or Gentile in whom Christ is, is itself glory, and the riches of glory; and so the Christian has a wealth of glory even now, in his thoughts and feelings.

What is the glory of this hoping? A feeling of hope cannot but shine in the reflected rays of the thing hoped for; especially so if the hope be in no danger of disappointment. If one hope for earthly riches or fame, and his hope be reasonably sure, his anticipations will have the same character of pleasure as belongs

to the possession of riches or fame. How
matchlessly blessed, then, must be that hoping, which has for its object *"the glory"* of
the Risen Church of the Glorified, and which
is not only reasonably sure, but *infallible* to
any one having Christ in him.

For what shall be the glory of the Church
of the glorified? The consummation of the
efficacy of all the work of Jesus Christ, God
manifest in the flesh. It shall consist in the
concentrated essence of Bethlehem, and Gethsemane, and Calvary; in the intended blessed
equivalent of that prodigious cry of desertion
which broke His own heart (Matt. xxvii. 46;
Ps. lxix. 20), and of that "loud voice" of victory which rent in twain the temple's veil
and made the earth quake (Matt. xxvii. 50,
51); in even the likeness to Himself, who is
the first fruits of them that have slept (1 John
iii. 2; 1 Cor. xv. 20). Can any possible effort
of the mind imagine a condition of human
being more glorious?

In particular, it shall be the glory of our
resurrection bodies; "sown in corruption,
raised in incorruption; sown in dishonor,
raised in glory; sown in weakness, raised in
power, sown a natural body raised a spiritual
body;" "bearing the image of the heavenly,"
and "fashioned like unto His glorious body";

making us equal to the angels (Luke xx. 36), and hence fitting us, like Gabriel, to range over the worlds of God's universe. It shall be the glory, too, of our new hearts in their unhindered development of Christly life, and thought, and love, and power; not, as now, repressed and harassed by association with our old corrupt hearts, and with our disordered bodies, but as freed from these entangling alliances, and served by the sublimer organs of our perfected bodies of the resurrection. It shall be the glory of our coming back with the Lord to the earth, and of sharing in the triumphs of His second appearing, amid the "glory of His Father and of the holy angels." It shall be the glory of the white-robed Elders on their thrones, and as sitting down with Christ in his throne, even as He is set down with His Father in His throne (Rev. iii. 21; iv. 4). The glory of the Living Creatures, too, in their executive functions and their attributes of greatness; their many wings, their eyes of intuition, before and behind, and all over them, their lion-like majesty, their far-sightedness and swiftness of motion like as of eagles, and yet their sympathies and feelings manlike (Rev. iv. 6-8; v. 8, 9). The glory of being to the Millennial Church as well-ministering priests of Christ, as reigning kings (Rev.

v. 10; xx. 6). The glory of our oneness with the Lord Jesus made visible;
for, like as the sapphire, and the em-
erald, and the diamond shine brightest when
placed in the strongest light, so, by reason of
His light being of a brightness so superior as
that the sun himself shall be ashamed (Isa.
xxiv. 23), we, as reflecting His light, shall be
made ourselves to shine forth as the sun in the
kingdom of our Father (Matt. xiii. 43). And,
finally, the glory, which shall endure "to all the
generations of the age of the ages" (Eph. iii.
21); for when, at length, the Millennial Church
shall have been transferred to their places
among the glorified, then shall there be "a new
heaven and a new earth," and "the tabernacle
of God shall be with men, and He will dwell
with them, and they shall be His peoples, and
God Himself shall be with them. And
God shall wipe away every tear from their
eyes; and death shall be no more, neither sor-
row, nor crying, neither shall there be any
more pain; because the former things have
passed away" (Rev. xxi. 1-4).

Ah, but all that is in the dim future. It is all
so far away. What! Are we not required to be
looking and waiting for "the glorious appearing of the great God and our Saviour, Jesus
Christ?" (1 Cor. i. 7; 2 Thess. i. 7; Tit. ii. 13;

1 Pet. i. 13 ; 2 Pet. iii. 12-14). And are we not commanded to watch for the signs (Matt. xxiv. 14, 15)? How long were the Old Testament saints in expectancy, as regarded the coming of the seemingly impossible Virgin-Born? And at length did He not come according to the letter? But since that first coming only about nineteen centuries have passed, and even now what do we see? That at least one of the signs is strikingly near its fulfilment. There lacks not a very great deal of the Gospel having been "preached in all the world for a witness unto all nations." "Then shall the end come." No, the glory of the Risen Church cannot be so exceedingly far away. And besides, if we die before the Lord come, happy as we cannot but be if we are with Christ, yet even there shall we be looking forward to this great event, even as Christ Himself is now doing (Heb. x. 13 ; Rev. vi. 10).

Well, such being the glory hoped for, must it not give glory, and riches of glory, to the process of our hoping? If the Church of the glorified shall be forever a joy unutterable, is not the true hoping for it a foretaste of that joy? If light, and beauty, and grandeur, and sharing with Christ, and perfected blessedness in God, be the characteristics of that coming glory, will not the believing soul, while at rest in the Saviour, become the more exhilarated in his faith, and the happier in his sympathy with God's will, on account of becoming intelligent of this hope, and of carefully indulging it? Must he not the more truly appreciate the death and resurrection of Christ for sinners, seeing that the oneness he has with his atoning Substitute, so real a thing it is, is yet to merge in the oneness of heavenly glory? What content, and serenity, and delighting in Christ, and fellowship with God, are fostered and developed by this hope. How it lives above any reigning worldliness of feeling, and any viciousness of life, seeing that such things are degradations in the light of the glory which it has in view. What a wealth of beauty, and brightness, and power, is in the thoughts and feelings of that soul.

Oh, the glory of being a Christian! And will we forget it, and avert our eyes from it, and so become dazzled by the pleasures of sin for a season, or by the speculative errors of unresting and unsatisfied men, who are as utterly devoid of any happiness of assurance as Noah's dove was without an inch of dry ground on which to rest its feet! Ah, this sinful world may lure and bewilder us, but it can give no satisfaction to our immortal moral nature. Its glories are of another sort; sometimes good,

and to be enjoyed with thankfulness; sometimes bad, and only bad continually, and de-
structive to the enjoyers of them; but, even at
their best estate, supplemented by sin, and sor-
row, and disappointment, and calamity. In
fact, the curse of sin is upon all things here,
even the lower kingdoms of creation, echoing
back the miseries of the human. Our flowers
have their thorns (Gen. iii. 18), and the honey
of life is surrounded with stings.

> "In and about in a regal wood
>   The birds were full of April glee;
>   On a leafing elm a bold thrush stood,
>   Singing a song that was understood
>   By a mate on a neighboring tree.
>   But a cloud came over the regal wood,
>   In the scream of a frightened hare;
>   A hound pursued it, eager for blood;
>   A squirrel nigh me shook where it stood;
>   And I fancied the world less fair.
>   Then I rose to depart from the regal wood,
>   And saw in the grass that there lay
>   A glittering snake with a raven hood;
>   The sight of it cooled and curdled my blood;
>   I trembled; and went on my way."

Aye, but is your way that way of faith in
Christ which leads to the Church of the Glorified? God forbid that I should glory save in
Jesus Christ, the wisdom of God, and the
power of God.

17

THE WORK OF THE PREACHER

"Whom we preach, warning every man, and teaching every man in every wisdom, that we may have presented every man perfect in Christ; whereunto I also toil, striving according to His working which worketh in me in power" (i. 28, 29).

THE connection of these verses with those preceding is very plain. Not only was the mystery made known through Him, which fact constitutes the personal appeal of the preceding verses, but he and his associates actually preached according to that mystery. That truth was to them a living principle of action—the explanation of their whole life work. Should not this fact have its effect on the Colossians to preserve them from the misleading of false philosophy?

But more than this, the apostle's own devoted service for the truth had brought, and was bringing, upon him peculiar toils; in the midst of which, however, he was energized and supported by a Divine in-working in power, and was enabled to achieve great and glorious results. Thus a double personal appeal is presented, that is, both himself and they who

were associated with him preached this Christ
in the fulness of the revelation of the mystery,
and he in particular especially toiled in so doing. Should not the Colossians be both influenced and preserved by these strivings?

The theme suggested is the *Work of the
Preacher.*

I. The true preaching of Christ differen-
tiates the preacher from the world's thinkers.
"Whom WE Preach." This is emphatic and
contradistinctive. Concerning Paul, Timothy,
Epaphras and those associated with him, whatever else might be said of them, at all events
they stood out in marked contrast to the world's
teachers. They were by themselves. The
ground of their contradistinction was this, that
they preached Christ—*this Christ,* revealed in
the preceding verses. And this was the whole
of their preaching. It was not their own speculations that they preached, nor the ceremonies,
nor the works of the law for salvation, nor
humanitarianism, not angels, not saints. It
was this Christ they preached everywhere and
to all.

But this preaching of theirs was altogether
beyond the plane of worldly thinking, as such
preaching must always be. There is a way of
preaching in which Christ is frequently mentioned and held up to admiration, while yet

His name is spoken only on the dead level of merely human conceptions. The believer's co-crucifixion with Christ, for instance, and, consequently, his not being according to the flesh, but according to the Spirit, are not at all in the plane of the world's thinking. Now, such contradistinctions from the world as this should be the preacher's test of himself rather than popularity.

II. The true preaching of Christ is distinguished and identified by the several details of its processes.

(1) There is a *warning* of every man concerning the errors that are extant, concerning the deceptions of his own heart and the wiles of the devil. This warning includes the call to repentance, to a radical change of thought about himself, about God and about sin.

(2) There is a *teaching* of every man, and the teaching is not that of general declamation but only whatever is of the faith. These two words, therefore, "warning" and "teaching" correspond to practice on the one hand and doctrine on the other.

(3) This teaching of every man is *in every wisdom*—the wisdom which includes the simplicity in Christ and also the deep things of God; which includes simple belief, and also the fulness and presentness of salvation; which in-

cludes oneness with Christ, righteousness and
santification with Him, co-heirship with Him,
salvation and service.   Wisdom which includes
the teaching concerning the Church, Israel and
the nations.   In other words, the dispensational
relations of the truth (I. Cor. x. 32).

(4) This teaching is that every man *may
have been presented perfect in Christ.* In other
words, this is the aim and the proper results
of this preaching when it is accomplished.   The
apostle's desire is that he may have presented
every man perfect in Christ even now (I. Cor.
ii. 6) as well as hereafter.   That word *perfect*
is borrowed from the heathen mysteries, and
here appropriated to the Gospel; it is, therefore, in its use a condemnation of those mysteries.   The idea is that perfection is only to
be found in Christ, and not at all in the heathen
mysteries referred to.   Moreover, it is found
positively in Christ, and we are perfect in His
perfection—perfectly justified, perfectly sanctified, made perfectly meet for glory.   Now,
such is the only proper result of true preaching, and such is its only true aim.   Without
this aim Christ is not truly understood by the
preacher, and his preaching is defective.   But
such an aim can be carried out only by both
warning and teaching in accordance with all
that Christ is.

(5) Notice that this teaching or preaching is with regard to *every man*. That expression, "every man," is employed three times, and harmonizes with "every wisdom." Thus the apostle strikes at the Gnostic exclusiveness, emphasizing the point that in this wisdom of God in Christ there are no restrictions as to persons or subjects, that is, the whole Christ is preached to every man. Of course he would be guided by the varying needs of individuals, but every one to whom he had access he fully warned and fully taught; and every one who would accept the warning and teaching he presented to God perfect in Christ. He glories in this universality of Christ; he mentions it over and over. Christ is the sole perfection for man, and whoever receives Him is perfected, whether the penitent thief, or the Magdalene, or Saul of Tarsus. The entire glory of our perfection belongs to Christ, not at all to ourselves, our circumstances or our works. What an *"un"*-earthly earthly excellence this is! Every man, even the least, is addressed by this Gospel, and every subject, even the greatest, is thrown open to his thoughts. Such is true preaching.

III. This kind of preaching is the outcome of the preacher's toil through the working in him of the power of Christ. *"I also toiled."*

He does not mean to insinuate that others did
not toil, but simply to affirm that he did toil
peculiarly. The true preacher can never be
without toil, both intellect and heart must be
necessarily exercised in order to such preaching. Now the apostle's toils were due partly
to the fact that he did not preach an exclusive
gospel. It was not exclusive either with reference to the Gnostic teaching of wisdom or the
Jewish teaching of law and ceremony. Indeed,
Paul might have saved himself from half the
troubles of his life had he been more exclusive
than he was. In like manner the toils of the
preacher now come partly from the opposition
of men to this freeness and fulness of God's
grace in Christ.

But, again, the apostle's toils resulted in part
from the necessities of his own personal pre-
paration for the work of such preaching.
He needed to keep himself always in readiness.
The fact of his inspiration did not preclude
this necessity, that is, the necessity of study, of
devotion and of watchings, both of himself and
of opportunities. And to this day the toils of
the preacher are the same.

Thus Paul *strove* even as an agonist in the
lists; but he strove *according to Christ working in him,* that is, he not only had an assured
belief of that in-working, but he was actually

influenced by means of it. And it worked in him *in power*—the power of the Holy Spirit producing in him clear views of the truth, gracious affections towards those to whom he preached it, spiritual enjoyment on his own part, the strength of Divine sanction and the comfort cf conscious support. Hence there were results, sinners were brought to Christ, believers were established in the faith, and his own heart was greatly cheered.

Such was the apostle's appeal to the Colossians, and such is his appeal to us. Let us remember in the conclusion of this meditation that both preachers and people are in common responsible for the prevailing faultiness of preaching.

18

THE CONFLICT OF THE PREACHER

"For I would have you know what great conflict
I have for you and them in Laodicea, and for as
many as have not seen my face in the flesh; that
their hearts may be comforted, they being knit together in love and unto all riches of the full assurance of the understanding, unto the thorough knowledge of the mystery of God, Christ, in whom are
all the treasures of wisdom and knowledge hidden"
(ii. 1-3).

THE division of chapters in this case is very
unfortunate, as the apostle is here continuing the personal appeal with which
the first chapter draws to a close, only that now
he more strongly presses the fact of his conflict. He calls special attention to the thought
of how great it is, and also to the fact that he
is waging it for those whom he had never seen;
and all this in order that their hearts might be
comforted, and all that follows in the text. A
moving appeal this!

This, like the passage previously considered,
is a description by the apostle of his own
ministry. In the last two verses of the preceding chapter he has given us his first description

of that ministry, but in these verses he exhibits the subject from another point of view. There he had referred to his striving subordinately, here he enlarges upon it.

I. His ministry was a *conflict*. This conflict did not come upon him by reason of his persecutions and sufferings, although these may be included in his thought, but since he was now in prison his conflict must have consisted chiefly of his mental anxiety and prayers on their behalf. It was a spiritual conflict in other words, in his thoughts and feelings, in his faith and prayers, fighting before God with the powers of evil; these powers showing themselves in the initial errors of the Colossians. And his exercises of heart and mind were most intense, for he says, "What great conflict!"

This reveals him to us as one who possessed the clearest and most definite conceptions of the Gospel for himself, and one who was wholly and purely devoted to its proclamation. We feel deeply about the salvation of a personal friend, but Paul had never seen the Colossians. It was therefore his knowledge and love of the truth, his glorying of Christ as the Saviour of men that causes his conflict. His conflict was sublime, godlike; his anxiety spiritual and unearthly.

And, besides, he had this great conflict for those who were Christians. This is very noticeable. It was not specifically for the unconverted, though of course the work of conversion would be ultimately subserved by his promoting among Christians fulness of the blessing of the Gospel of peace; but the views and feelings of the already converted were what was causing him his great conflict. This again shows us his pure insight into the truth as God has revealed it. His earnest feeling and striving were not merely for conversions, but mainly for teaching and enforcing the whole counsel of God. So his conflict originated, and so it continued. We can easily see, therefore, of what kind were his constant thoughts, and how deep and pure and overflowing was his own gospel life. We get a peep into his prison sanctum, and we *hear* him thinking, living, joying, triumphing, praying, striving.

Now this ministry of Paul is the pattern of what every ministry should be. We cannot equal him, but we can follow him. The same dangers to the faith of Christians are as imminent now as then, and the same conflict in spirit is as imperative to the ministry of Christ.

II. Paul tells us not only that his ministry was a conflict, but the object he had in view in the conflict. This object was to preserve and promote the fulness of the Gospel truth among believers. This is evident from the repeated statements in this passage, and from the whole tenor of it. By his earnest solicitude, his importunate prayers and the work of his inspired pen, even in prison, his purpose was to bring Christians into the clearness of Gospel doctrine and under its abounding power, but, in order to accomplish this, his object branched out into various particulars:

(1) "That their hearts *may be comforted.*" In the comforting of the heart by the truth, the truth itself is secured. The consolation of the feelings is a great clarifier of the intellect, since it presupposes a genuine personal sympathy with the subject, and is, in that sense, as eye-sight to the thoughts of the mind. It might seem that *strengthened* would have been a better word than "comforted," because the result sought was the steadfastness of the Colossians against all error, but the very thought of the passage is that comfort is strength. (See Neh. viii. 10, and John xv. 11.) Indeed, even in secular studies, if one is not in sympathy with the subject, he will make poor progress in its understanding, and so a man may theoretically receive every doctrine of the Gospel, but if he be not himself comforted thereby, he may fall

an easy prey to the archers of error. Thus it is explained that so many evangelical believers are fascinated and taken captive by the perverted phraseology of so-called evangelical teaching.

Paul would have every believer comforted by his Gospel belief, entering consciously into a feeling of its reality and all-pervading sense of its sweetness. The comfort, consolation, joy—this he here teaches is the attainable blessedness of every believer and, in fact, is their safety. Moreover, he teaches that it may be habitually and aboundingly his conscious possession, for he uses the Aorist subjunctive, *"may have been comforted"*—may have been all along through the past, may have been as looking back from any given time, may have been continuously, that is, accustomed to the comfort. This is one of the leading senses of the great Aorist tense, and suggests to us in this case the constant joy of consolation. This is comfort, strength and freeness against error.

So the apostle labored to build his believers into a solid bulwark against heresy and all doctrinal falsehood; and no ministry is true to its God-given aim which does not preach this happy privilege and duty of believers and urge it upon them, and endure a mighty conflict before God to make them comforted, and therefore the always triumphant holders of the truth in the midst of a gainsaying world.

(2) That they be *"knit together in love."* The love here means not the love of unrenewed or unregenerated human nature, but the sense of God's love of us in Christ. Such love is a knitting together of hearts, the oneness of all in Christ. And such knitting together of hearts becomes a solid phalanx in the service of divine truth, for two or more are better than one.

The knitting together of heart to heart acts and reacts upon each one's personal sympathies with the truth, and therefore multiplies the comfort in the soul, enlarging and consolidating the strength. Error is *many,* and therefore sooner or later is disruption; but truth, while having many sides and aspects, is but *one* definite reality. Now, when we are knit together in that love which comes only from a sense of the truth, we continue to hold together, and the truth is kept and honored. This knitting together, therefore, is also included in the aim of every true ministry, nor is any ministry discharging its God-given aim except as it is enduring a conflict before God for accomplishing so important a result. It is to be labored for in clear teaching, in earnest prayer and in the cultivation of the brotherhood in Christ.

(3) That they be so knit together *"unto all riches of the full assurance of the understanding."* They are knit together *in* love, but *unto* all the riches referred to. These riches are the consequences of being knit together in love. The understanding referred to is, of course, a correct understanding; that is, an understanding of the Gospel such as is exactly according to the reality. "The full assurance of the understanding" is an understanding without mistiness or confusion, or distortion—the established consciousness that we do see the Gospel clearly.

Thus we see the Bible reveals the fact that its teachings are definite, and precise and easily to be ascertained. And moreover, that every man is without excuse who is not himself definite, distinct, clear and settled. Now the contrary of this is what is often contended for by many, but the true preacher will stand with Paul upon this question, that is, he will endure a great conflict before God rather than surrender the cause of that definite, clear assured understanding among his people. Love never compromises the truth. It is compassionate to the errorist, but gives no allowance to the error.

Now if a sense of God's love in Christ be cultivated and enjoyed, if the comfort of the gospel abounds in our hearts, we cannot but

attain to the full assurance of the understanding.   In such a path there are no insuperable
obstacles.   It is simply the fleshly pride of
opinion, the duskiness of worldly thinking that
makes difficult the full reception of the truth.
Love is itself intelligence, divine intelligence.
Joy is a burst of sunlight from heaven, and the
happy, rejoicing believer, giving full scope to
his existing conceptions of the truth, will open
his soul to the deeper things of scripture and to
God's blaze of daylight, as the flower expands
to the sun in the heavens.   In other words, it is
as we live up to the truth we now have that we
receive more truth.

And how blessed a thing is the full assurance of the understanding!   It has riches—
all riches.   Is there anything richer than the
satisfaction of looking a subject through and
through?   Not merely as philosophers analyze
and apprehend it, but as fully understanding it
in its reality.   This is light, this is pleasure,
this is settledness, this is directness, this is energy.   This assurance of understanding is the
ground of the assurance of faith, and the assurance of faith is the ground of the assurance
of hope.   In this combination of assurances
what ineffable blessedness there is!   It is heaven condensed.   It is the morning of the eternal noon.   Such an assured understanding is

immovable in the midst of false teaching, and at the same time is connected with a genuine humility.

To lead believers to this assurance of understanding is another feature of the God-given purpose of the ministry, and to accomplish this purpose there must be a conflict of solicitude, and thorough thinking, and earnest praying on the part of the preacher in the presence of God.

(5) That they come *"unto the thorough knowledge of the mystery of God, Christ, in Whom are all the treasures of wisdom and knowledge hidden."* This principle is only a repetition of the preceding one, employing different language, however, and bringing to bear another set of illustrations. "The mystery of God" is here explained as being "Christ, in Whom are all the treasures hidden." Therefore the thorough knowledge of the mystery of God is "thorough knowledge of Christ." Christ is the mystery of God because of having been revealed to us, for, if He had not been revealed, we could never have known Him. He is, however, specifically, the mystery of God because in Him are all the treasures of wisdom and knowledge hidden. The treasures of knowledge include our conception of truth, and the treasures of wisdom our appreciation of that knowledge, its relations, its uses, its re-

sources, its practical applications. All are in
Him, but hidden in Him. In Him they are
compacted, expanded, guarded, preserved, and
in Him only. They are hidden in Him, but He
Himself is revealed. As we get Him, then,
we get them, for He is the treasure-box of
God. Now the thorough knowledge of Christ
as containing all this in Himself, the clear understanding of it, and the going on to understand it more and more, according to the revelation—this is the full assurance of the understanding. This is riches, all riches, treasure,
all treasures. And to bring believers into such
thorough knowledge is another aspect of the
God-given purpose of the ministry. But what
a conflict it implies, and what appreciation on
the part of the minister himself!

19

THE FULL DOCTRINE OF CHRIST

"And this I say, in order that no one may beguile you by false reasoning in persuasive discourse. For though I am verily absent in the flesh, on the contrary, I am with you in the spirit, joying and beholding your orderly array, and the solid front of your faith unto Christ. As then you received the Christ, Jesus the Lord, in Him walk; having been rooted and being built up in Him: and being established in the faith, as ye were taught, abounding therein in thanksgiving" (ii. 4-7).

IN the preceding verses, the apostle had spoken of two things: the full truth of Christ, and his own conflict for the Christians of Colossæ in the interests of that truth, and now he reviews what went before with the express purpose of putting them on their guard against departing from that truth. The text, therefore, forms a kind of transition from the first to the second part of the epistle, which is polemic in its character.

In this transition it is stated that our reception of the full doctrine of Christ is the only and sufficient safeguard against error; also that he felt the deepest interest in their condition as they stood related to that doctrine, and finally, he would have them intent upon using and enjoying what they had gained by it. The first thought is the teaching of the fourth verse, the second of the fifth, and the third of the sixth and seventh verses of the text.

First, let us look at what he says concerning the full doctrine of Christ as the only and sufficient safeguard against error. What he says indeed seems like a truism, but let us remember, nevertheless, that it is only full assurance of understanding, considered in our previous lecture, which will so protect us. Error is easily coined into the likeness of truth, and only a thorough knowledge of the mystery of God can always enable us to detect it.

Second—This truth of Christ, he teaches us, should be administered most definitely, earnestly, wisely and lovingly. He puts himself forward as an example in the doing of this very thing, and in that becomes the type of the ministry. The ministry is set for the defence of the Gospel, not only as against the infidel, but as expounding the Word to them that believe.

In this connection, observe Paul's testimony to his joy in beholding their order and faith towards Christ, thus calling attention to the good that was among them, for their comfort. That expression, "joy and beholding" is peculiar. Joying at what? At the orderly array? But then should not "beholding" have come first? No, there is no need of supposing a logical inversion here, for he evidently means that he was joying at the orderly array already observed, and that he was still beholding it because he was joying in it. And notice the words *"orderly array,"* which means each one in his place, submissive to discipline, submissive to them that are over them in the Lord, no self-will, no isolated action. *A solid front of faith unto Christ.* Order and faith are thus united, and the provision of either without the other marks an unprosperous church, for in that case the one becomes formalism and the other fanaticism. But where the two are really united, there is prosperity, and where there is such prosperity, the church may be wisely commended for it. Here is a lesson for all pastors, and for parents as well, to commend that in Christ which is commendable.

But Paul opens a further way into their hearts for his teachings by reminding them so lovingly that though absent in the flesh from them, he was with them in spirit, i. e., in thought, affection and sympathy.

Third—He closes this section of the epistle

with a practical exhortation to use and enjoy all that they have in Christ, and it may be remarked in passing, that the joy of the cause is always its strength.

He exhorts them, for example, to "walk in Christ as they had received Him." First— They *had* received Him. They had received *Him;* not merely a truth concerning Him. It is by means of the truth that He is received, but He, Himself, is what is received. It is a person whom we apprehend by faith, and then He comes into our hearts. We receive Him once for all. We receive Him as the Christ, i. e., the Messiah promised. We receive Him as Jesus, the Saviour of us from our sins, and we receive Him as Lord, the Master of our wills, conscience and affections. The true doctrine of the Christ, then, is first, the historic recognition of Jesus, and second, the acceptance of Him as the Lord (1:15-20).

Now as we received Christ so are we to use Him. We are to realize that we received Him, and therefore, use Him: and the very same way in which we received Him, is the way in which we should use Him: i. e., in the same simplicity, and according to our first teachings concerning Him (2:7).

We are to use Him by *walking in* Him. Observe that He, Himself, is the Path. It is not the teaching concerning Him which is the path, but He, Himself.   We walk in Him. All our energies are put forth as consciously in Him.

And such walking is attended by several things, as, for example, *"having been rooted in Him"*: i. e., grounded in Him at the first, and knowing that we were so grounded. This "rooting" is equivalent to our having been put into Christ by means of the simplest fundamental principles of the gospel.

"And being built up in Him."   Here is the idea of increasing as the result of having been rooted.   In I. Cor. 3:10-14, we have the thought of being built up upon Christ as our foundation, but here we have the thought of being built up in Christ, as the cementing element.   He is our conscious cement.   And the true growth is that of this conscious oneness with Christ.

And we are not only being built up in Him, but also *"established in the faith as ye were taught."*   Notice the expression " as ye were taught," for it is only as the old true faith is more and more understood and assured, that we grow in Him.

Finally, we are not only established in the faith, but *"abounding"* in it in *"thanksgiving."* In other words thanksgiving is the element in

which faith becomes plentiful and abundant,
and without it faith cannot grow.   Thanksgiving is the end of all human conduct, and is as
the farmer's crop which laughs in thankfulness
for the toil of the plow.   It is the grand refrain of this epistle.   See 1 :3, 2 :7, 3 :15, 17
and 4 :2.

Such is the walking in Christ and its several
accompaniments.   What an organic connection we have here!   And notice the play of the
tenses—Ye *did* receive, now *walk; having been*
rooted; *being* built up; *being* established as
you *were* taught; *abounding*.   How much theology is here!   And notice also the rapid
change of metaphors in this language, walk,
rooted, built up.   Christ is the Path, Christ
is the Soil, Christ is the Foundation, Christ is
the cement.   On the other hand, the Christian
is the walker, the tree, the building; he is ever
in motion and yet ever at rest.

20

THE EMPTY DECEITS OF MEN

"Beware lest there shall be any one that is leading you away as his prey by means of philosophy and empty deceit, according to the traditions of men, according to the rudiments of the world, and not according to Christ. Because in Him dwelleth in bodily fashion, permanently, all the fulness of the Godhead" (ii. 8, 9).

AT this point we enter upon the strictly polemic matter of the epistle, to which we have been conducted by a gentle transition. After dwelling upon the pure doctrine of Christ, we are now to consider a specification of particular errors of men.

First, notice the description here given of philosophy. "Of philosophy and empty deceit": i. e., *the* philosophy which is empty deceit. In other words, the Colossian heresy in particular. Paul does not characterize all philosophy in these terms, but only such as is empty deceit. This word, philosophy, had a noble origin, for it is said to have arisen out of the humility of Pythagoras, who called himself the *"lover* of wisdom." Now, however, it had degenerated into the meaning of subtle reasonings and profitless speculations. And it is remarkable that this is the only instance of the use of this word in the New Testament. Here it is used as the boasted term of the teachers of error. The apostle discarded it from his own vocabulary, and did not attempt to Christianize it as has been done with so many other words.

And, moreover, he enables us to ascertain just what philosophy, in other words, what reasonings and speculations of men are—only empty deceit. Such are they which are according to the tradition of men, resting alone on tradition, and having no support from revelation. He strikes especially at the esoteric doctrine of the Gnostics which had no historic books open to all the world, and teeming with facts of God's own teaching, like the Scriptures. All such speculations are empty deceipt. They are "not according to Christ," but according to the rudiments of the world.

The word "world" has various meanings in the Scripture, to be determined, usually, by the context. In this case, however, by comparing Gal. 4:3 and 9 with verse 11 of the present chapter, it would appear that by the "world," the apostle means, first, the material, external, sensuous, visible world, and second, that by "rudiments of the world," or elementary les-

sons of the world, he means such as are taught
by the Levitical ritual; a ritual, that is, which
is regarded as necessary to salvation; for such
was the idea of the false teachers, and such the
relation of the Mosaic ritual. Paul implies
this also in his arguments to be dealt with later,
in verses 16-23, of this chapter. But Paul's
use of "rudiments of the world" applies not
only to the Levitical ordinances, but also to all
other ceremonial observances, as we may
gather from the fact that false teachers had
added their own inventions to the Mosaic pre-
scriptions, and also from the phrase "which
sort of things," which we find in the 23d verse,
already referred to. Now these rudiments, or
elementary lessons, of the world are an "empty
deceit." Even those of the Levitical ritual,
though that ritual was instituted of God, are
an empty deceit, for now Christ has come, and
has done away with them. They are not according to Christ, they are not according to the
soul's experience of union with Christ, and are
for those reasons an empty deceit. He, Himself, is the region of the soul's conscious spirituality, and life, and thought, and enjoyment.
These are above the region of ritualism.

Second—After the apostle describes the
philosophy of the world, he proceeds to set
forth the true wisdom of God in the words

"because in Him dwelleth permanently, in bod-
ily fashion, all the fulness of the Godhead."
That word "because" is emphatic, as though
Paul would say, He, Christ, is Himself of necessity the true wisdom.   Notice the word
Godhead here.   It is a translation of the
Greek word *theotés,* which means Deity.   In
Rom. i. 20 it translates *theiotês:* two very different words, it will be perceived, the latter
meaning divinity, the former Deity.   The
Latin fathers finding in their language only
the word *divinitas,* coined from the word Deus,
the word Deitas, which means Deity absolute and essential, and this is the word here
used.   Let it not be overlooked that the "fulness" of Deity dwelt in Christ.   The
apostle said this in view of the Gnostic teaching that the various emanations
of Deity had only *something* of Deity
in them.   Christ had its fulness.   Could there
be a stronger possible assertion of Christ as
God?   And this fulness of the Deity dwelt in
Him in *bodily fashion*: i. e. in Him as having
a human body on earth, and still now in heaven.   A teaching this which reminds us of
John I. 1 and 14.   And this fulness of Deity
dwelleth in Him *permanently,* and not tran-
siently.   Cerinthus taught that the *pleroma,* or
"fulness," came on Christ at His baptism, and
left Him before He died on the cross, but Paul

says it was permanently in Him. This word permanently, though not expressed in our English version, is the very thought or word of the apostle.

All this being so, therefore, Christ is the true wisdom. Whoever has Christ has God. Whoever desires to add something of his own to Christ, desires more than God. Therefore, whatever is not according to Christ is an empty deceit.

Third—All this gives occasion for the exhortation, "beware": i. e. take heed, in view of what are empty deceits of men, and of what Christ is. There is danger of being led away captive, and as a prey, you, yourself, your body (see vs. 16), and soul (18), through ritualism and heresy.

And mark it well, that this exhortation is given, notwithstanding, the condition of the Colossian believers, as stated in 1:12, 13, for it is by such warnings that God keeps us to the end as His elect. Paul here acts on the maxim *obsta principiis*, "resist the beginnings." This church was in an excellent condition but error threatened, and had begun to act. He would oppose the very beginnings of error, and, when we see how vigorously he wages opposition to it, should we not be impressed with the exceeding urgency of like watchfulness?

21

FULNESS IN CHRIST

"And ye are in Him having been filled full, who is the Head of every principality and power. In whom also ye were circumcised with circumcision not made with hand, in the putting off of the body of the flesh, in the circumcision of Christ, buried together with Him in the baptism. In whom also ye were raised together with Him through the faith of the operation of God, who raised Him from among the dead" (ii. 10-12).

E VERY philosophy is an empty deceit which is not according to Christ, " because in Him dwelleth in bodily fashion, permanently, all the fulness of the Godhead." Not only so, but true believers are *in* Christ and are filled full. Why then should they be led astray by false teaching? Such is the connection with the preceding verses, while all the other words of this text are but an amplification of this its first sentence.

Let us consider this first sentence in detail, which is one of the richest in the Word of God, a summary of the whole of Ephesians, and, indeed, of the whole Gospel.

"Ye are in Him."   Observe that he says this
of all the true believers in Colossæ, no matter
what their different personal attainments in
holy living were.   Believers are in Christ as
their substitute, and the identity is to be considered as an organic one, mysterious but real.
See for example such passages as Rom. 8:1-3
and Gal. 2:20.   It is the judicial condition of
the believer: i. e. God's estimate of him who is
pardoned, justified and made righteous in
Christ.   God sees the believer only in Christ,
and never as outside of Him; identified with
Him in all His atoning work.

"Having been filled full."   The believer
is filled full in Christ because he, himself, is in
Christ, and Christ is in Him.   The order of
thought is that we are in Christ because He is
in us, but the order of fact is that He is in us
before we are in Him, for we are dead, and He
must become our life before we believe.   Christ
then is in us, and we are filled with Him, with
His merits, His righteousness, His preciousness, His life, His sonship, His heirship, His
glory.   See Rom. 8:10-18; 28-39.   We are
filled full, possessing the fulness of His salvation.   Every believer, at the moment he becomes a believer, is thus filled.   It is done.
He is filled.   He has it all as his own.   He
may not consciously possess it or enjoy it,

which is growth in grace; but nevertheless, it
is all his, and his growth in grace must start
forth and continue out of the conviction that
it is all his even now. This conviction, if
clear and intelligent, will save him from many
perversions of scripture, and practical confu-
sions on the subject of sin in daily life.

Second—Let us look at the inspired amplification of this first sentence of our text.

*"Who is the head of every principality and
power."* This evidently was intended to teach
that the believer required no other mediator
such as any of the angels, as the Gnostics
taught.

*"In Whom also ye were circumcised with cir-
cumcision not made with hand, in the putting
off of the body of the flesh in the circumcision
of Christ, buried together with Him in the baptism."* This is intended to show that there
was no need of a ritual circumcision, as the
false teachers taught, inasmuch as they had
the spiritual substance of it in Christ. In
other words, so filled were they in Him, that
they possessed all that was symbolized by that
right. The circumcision was not made with
hand. It was a spiritual thing. A circumcision of the heart, and the real substance of
the physical right. It was the "putting off of
the body of the flesh," the realization of that

which the other circumcision symbolized. And notice that it was a putting off, not of a part, but of the whole body of the flesh: i. e. the corrupt nature itself. It is all ruined, and it is all put off in Christ. And this is a real thing in Christ—the believer died. Moreover, it is the "circumcision of Christ": i. e., it is not done by rights or efforts of our own, but in what Christ has provided and confirmed. The idea is carried still further in the thought that we are "buried together with Him in the baptism." The meaning is, that we were circumcised in Christ when we were thus buried in the baptism. But now, what baptism is meant? Not baptism with water, surely? For as the circumcision is spiritual, so the baptism must be spiritual. The baptism by the *Holy Ghost* is the ruling baptism of the New Testament, and is always to be understood except where the language or context makes evident the contrary. Indeed, Rom. 6:4 shows what the baptism is, namely, the baptism into death. The being baptized into anything is the being brought under, and saturated with its influence and power. When we were circumcised in Christ, it was by means of getting under the power of His death so really and thoroughly that we were buried with Him, lying in the same grave. The realization of the full symbolism of circumcision is in our dying with Christ, and thus putting off the body of the flesh. This is the purity set forth in circumcision, and the purity we have in Christ.

"In Whom also ye were raised together with Him through the faith of the operation of God, Who raised Him from among the dead." At the same time the believer was circumcised and put to death in Christ, he was also raised together with Him. Raised in the life of Christ. Our resurrection, therefore, has in part already taken place, thus the identity with Christ continues, and this is through faith in God's operation as raising Him from among the dead, and not through philosophy and vain deceit.

22

TRIUMPH IN CHRIST

"Even you, being dead in your transgressions and uncircumcision of your flesh, He quickened you together with Him, forgiving us all our transgressions, blotting out the handwriting against us in ordinances which were hostile. And He hath taken it out of the way, nailing it to the cross; stripping off and away from Himself the principalities and powers, He made a show of them boldly, leading them in triumph in it" (ii. 13-15).

THE connection here with the preceding language is very plain. *"Even you."* Yes, you, though Gentiles, may consider this truth as applying to you as well as to the Jews.

First, then, let us consider what God does in and through Christ for the soul He saves.

(1) By nature that soul is dead in transgressions which are distinct acts of sin; and dead, not only in transgressions, but in the uncircumcision of the flesh, which, as we have seen before, points to the absolute corruption and ruin of the nature; in other words, sin in

principle as well as in act. The context clearly shows that he is here speaking, not only of the condition of these Gentiles physically, but morally as well. The physical fact of circumcision was simply symbolical of their utter corruption in the sight of God. They were dead both in nature and in acts.

(2) The first thing that God does in grace to the dead soul is to quicken it together with Christ, giving it life—an act of merciful sovereignty. As this life is in and with Christ, it indicates the vital and organic character of His substitution on behalf of guilty men. Observe the use of the aorist tense in the verb "quickened," which indicates that this work of grace was done at a definite point of time, i.e., the moment the soul believed on Christ.

(3) Not only does God quicken the soul in Christ, but forgives it all its transgressions, graciously and freely taking away condemnation. Compare Luke vii. 42.

(4) And He not only forgives all transgressions, but furthermore, blots out the handwriting against us in ordinances, a truth which carries on the idea of forgiveness, illustrating it under the figure of a debt. The word "handwriting" here is that used almost entirely for the autograph on a promissory note or bond, and frequently occurs in the Roman law books.

It was handwriting *"against us,"* i.e., the identical handwriting to which our particular signature was attached. "The ordinances" or decrees are God's decrees, such as the ten commandments, the ceremonial law, and the law written in our moral nature. It is in these decrees that we find our own handwriting that is against us, for we assent to the fact that the law is good, and that it is our obligation to obey it. It has, nevertheless, become hostile to us, exceedingly active and persistent in opposition to us on account of our own sin. But God blots it out, cancels the bond, erases the signature, pays the debt. And this He does in and through Jesus Christ, "Who His own self bare our sins in His own body on the tree" (I. Pet. ii. 24, 25).

Second. Let us consider what is meant by this which God does for the soul He saves.

(1) Christ hath taken the handwriting out of the way. It is, therefore, not only erased, as we have seen, but the document itself is removed and remains away.

(2) More than this. He has nailed it to the cross, and thus not only taken it away, but destroyed it. The nailing of the document was practically the nailing of Himself to the cross, for "He bare our sins." Compare Galatians vi. 14. What an expression of substitution

this is, and how thoroughly and eternally are the sins of God's people forgiven!

(3) He stripped off and away from Himself the principalities and powers, by which is meant the evil principalities and powers. See Ephesians vi. 12. They seized on His human nature, which, though without sin, had infirmities, as we see illustrated in the temptation in the wilderness, and the agony of Gethsemane as well as that of Calvary. But His victory was complete, for the powers of evil which had clung to His humanity were turned off and cast aside forever. Now that victory is the victory of the believing soul, and we become circumcised in the putting off of the body of the flesh, even as He stripped off from Himself these principalities and powers. He rose from the dead in a humanity free from all infirmity, and which these powers can never touch again. And so have we risen in and with Him in the life eternal.

(4) Moreover, He made a show of these powers boldly, openly, confidently, exhibiting them to the whole universe.

(5) Finally, He led them in triumph in the cross, triumphing in their helplessness, the cross itself being the sphere of the triumph. Thus we have the paradox of the crucifixion, and the cross becomes the victor's triumphant car before the eyes of the universe.

23

THE PRACTICAL WARNING

"Let not any one therefore judge you in eating or in drinking, or in respect of a holy day, or of new moon, or of Sabbaths; which are a shadow of things to come; but the body is of Christ" (ii. 16, 17).

AS we have seen from the preceding chapter, the bond is canceled, the law of ordinances is repealed, and, therefore, on the basis of this fact, the Christians at Colossæ are here warned not to be brought into bondage thereto again. As with circumcision, so it is with all the other ordinances, those of eating and drinking, and those connected with the observances of sacred times— all these things are but a shadow of things to come, while the body is of Christ. The apostle is here striking at the *practical error* of the false teachers in this church as expressed in their excessive ritualism and rigorous æstheticism; their theological error is attacked in the verses following.

First, let us notice the things enumerated in this warning. Eating and drinking, for ex-

ample, were indeed referred to in the Mosaic
law, though little was said upon the latter of
the two, scarcely anything that could affect the
ordinary every-day life of the people. But
these false teachers went far beyond the law in
this respect, as they did in other places than
Colossæ, judging from the allusion of the
apostle in his letters to the Romans and to
Timothy. See Romans xiv. 2 and I. Timothy
iv. 2, 3. The "sacred" times included such
annual holy days as the Passover, Pentecost,
etc. The "new moon" was a monthly period,
referred to in Numbers x. 10 and xxviii. 11;
the "Sabbaths," of course, were weekly. As to
this last named "sacred time"—the Sabbath—
the apostle is speaking only and expressly of it
from the Jewish point of view. It is the
Jewish Sabbath as such, the keeping of which
he warns against. The Sabbath as expressive
of the law of creation, and as supplying the
principle which underlies the fourth command-
ment, he does not here include. His own ob-
servance of the Lord's Day and other recogni-
tions of it in the New Testament would seem
to be satisfying upon this point.

Secondly, let us consider the nature of the
warning concerning these things. The apostle
does not merely say "do not observe these
things"; he does say that, indeed, and very

much more. He says, do not let anyone
judge you with regard to these things, let no
one take you to task or call you to account concerning them. Let them not make such things
a basis of judgment as regards your standing
in Christ. Deny the right of any one to judge
you in this way, since they who would thus
judge you, violate the principles of the Gospel,
the work of Christ having taken away the ap-
plicability of such things to you (I. Cor. viii.
8).

Thirdly, let us observe the reiterated reason
for this warning. Verse 17, for example, presents the condensed embodiment of the teaching which has preceded, and presents the subject under a new illustration. For example,
such things are a shadow. They are unsub-
stantial. The shadow is cast in advance of the
things to come, and is its type, but nevertheless, the type is only a shadow after all. See
Hebrews x. i. The many shadows of the Levitical system are only one great shadow when
they are considered altogether, and just as the
shadow proves the existence of the object
which forecasts it, so the whole Levitical system demonstrates the truth of the Gospel.

"But the body is of Christ." The body, i.e.,
the things to come. They are a solid good.
Their very shadow attests it. The body in

this case is the Gospel. It is that which stands in the light of the personal Christ and casts a shadow. It is He who gives light and efficacy to the Gospel revelation, and we enjoy the Gospel only as we are in union with Him. The ancient Jew took the shadow as foretelling the body, but the modern ritualist, alas, takes the shadow instead of the body.

24

THE DOCTRINAL WARNING

"Let no one beguile you of the prize, taking delight in humility and worship of the angels, standing on the things which he hath seen, vainly puffed up by the mind of his own flesh. Not holding fast the Head from whom all the body, by means of the joints and bands being supplied and knit together, increaseth with the increase of God" (ii. 18, 19).

WE have here a description of one whose views concerning the truth are diametrically opposite to those taught by the apostle, especially in verses 9 and 10; and against whom, as a dangerous robber or beguiler, we are to be on our guard. His description includes the following things:

(1) He takes "delight in humility and worship of the angels." "Humility" in this case is used ironically, the idea being that Christ is too high for these false teachers, and they must have lower beings, such as the angels, for mediators. It is the mock-humility of the Roman Catholic and Greek Churches, for example, and is in its very nature insidiously attractive.

(2) He stands "on the things which he hath seen." In other words, he does not stand by faith or walk by it, but rather in accordance with his own visual experience, and from his own inferences and observations in the realm of sight. The idea is this—that just as a poor and uninfluential man cannot go into the presence of a king, though that king be a fellow mortal, except some one introduce him, so Christ, although a God-man, is too high for human fellowship, except through lower mediation. The utter opposition of such teaching to the revelation of divine grace has already been sufficiently set forth in the preceding chapters.

(3) He is "vainly puffed up by the mind of his own flesh." The word "flesh" here does not mean the body merely, but the whole of unrenewed human nature, the mind as well as the body, the whole of which "flesh" is corrupt. See John iii. 6. The mind, of course, includes the understanding and the thoughts, a consideration bearing upon the meaning of repentance, which involves and makes necessary a change of mind. The words "puffed up" are very noticeable as sustaining the conception of the mock-humility in this case, which is really pride and vanity of the clearest kind. It is paralleled in a sense by the slowness of the

awakened sinner to come to Christ. It is not humility that detains him, but fleshly vanity and pride, though he may be unconscious of it at the time.

(4) "He does not hold fast the Head." Of course, the Head in this case refers to Christ, as we have seen in verse 10. And holding "fast the Head" refers to the possession of strong, clear and definite views concerning Christ, as He is thus revealed to us in the Word of God. Such a holding of Christ does not admit of mock-humility.

(5) Accordingly, this false teacher here described, as well as any follower of his, is not a member of that body, which "by means of the joints and bands being supplied and knit together increaseth with the increase of God." In other words, he is not a member of the true Church of Christ, his views of Scripture truth, and his mental condition precluding him therefrom. Nor should one who is a member of the Church, or the body of Christ, suffer himself to be misled by one who is outside thereof.

Now what is this body of which Christ is the head? It is first of all an organic society, as indicated by the use of the word "body." In the next place it is a *vital* organism drawing life from its Head, there being oneness of body and Head, both possessing the same life.

Now there is interdependence of body and head, for if you separate them, both will die; hence there is a sense, therefore, in which even Christ cannot be the Christ except as being connected with the saved ones, the members of His body.

There is also intercommunion in the body. There are joints and bands. There are joinings and ligaments, showing the dependence of the members one upon another.

But there is communion with Christ by means of this intercommunion in the body, as the figure of a human body illustrates. Indeed, on the principle of Christ's being the Second Adam, He is the Saviour of any one soul only because He is the Saviour of other souls. As far as we know, no angel has ever been the parent of offspring, so that if a Saviour had been provided for the fallen angels, it must have been upon a different principle altogether.

This body increaseth with the increase of God, i.e., it groweth with the growth of God— growth in God's life, God's thoughts, God's will, a consideration this, which implies the Deity of Christ, since the life by which the body grows is life derived from the Head.

After considering this description of the false teacher and his teachings, let us dwell a moment upon the warning. "Let no one beguile you of the prize." My fellow believer, you are running a race, there is a prize for you, but there is danger of being beguiled or robbed of it. And it is by reason of your sense of responsibility in this matter that God keeps you to eternal life. Be not cheated of the special reward of faithful service. Hold fast the Head, and appreciate your superiority in Christ to every false teacher.

25

THE FALSE ASCETICISM

"If ye died with Christ from the rudiments of
the world, why, as though living in the world, do
ye subject yourselves to ordinances, handle not,
neither taste, nor touch (which things are all of them
for destruction in the using up), according to the
commandments and doctrines of men? Which sort
of things have a reputation indeed of wisdom in will-
worship, and humility and unsparingness of the body,
not in any value as to indulgence of the flesh" (Col.
ii. 20-23).

IN this text the apostle, having given his
warning as to the theology of the false
teachers, now returns to their ethical practice, in other words, their asceticism, for there
was a close connection between their theology
and their ethics.

First. *We have here a description of the
Christian.* He is one who has died with Christ
from the rudiments of the world. This, indeed, is stated in the form of an argument, and
as an argument the statement is positive and
absolute. *He died with Christ.* A death which
was effected at a definite moment in time past,

as the word "died" in the aorist tense indicates. That time past was, in the mind of God, when Christ Himself died upon the cross. But practically, so far as the believer is concerned, it occurred the moment he accepted Christ by faith as his personal Saviour. For other allusions to the believer's position as dying with Christ, see Romans vi. 8, 11, II. Timothy ii. 11, as well as Colossians i. 11, 12, already considered.

He died with Christ *from the rudiments of the world;* that is, from all ceremonial observances. But, it may be asked, how did Christ die in this regard? In two senses at least. First, as having been "made under the law," He was bound to the fulfilment of these observances, and their fulfilment on behalf of the believer, and thus, when He died, He died from them. Secondly, these observances were all fulfiled in His death, in the sense that He was the substance of which they were the shadow, and in His death, therefore, they were abolished. Now, the false teachers had added to these Mosaic requirements, but their additions were also included in the "rudiments of the world." Christ's dying from them, therefore, must have included all ceremonial observances in their very nature, whether divine or human. We thus see that His death settled completely and forever the question of sin, so far as the believer is concerned. Nothing could now intrude as the procuring cause of perfect pardon. All ordinances are impertinent and an infringement of the efficacy of His work. By His death He secured the creating of a new life in the believer by the Holy Spirit, by which He is brought into fellowship with God, so that no ordinances of any kind whatsoever, whether of the treatment of the body, or the worship of angels, or any other thing, are needed to bridge over the distance between God and him. The new life is Christ's life, and in it we are one with God Incarnate. To *die from* is a very remarkable phraseology, and means that as Christ died once and finally, so has dying separated Him forever from all such things. But the believer, as we have seen, died with Christ. He died with Christ *to sin.* Romans vi. 2; *to self,* II. Corinthians v. 15; *to the law,* Galatians vi. 14.

But in this connection it may be asked: How about the ordinances of Baptism and the Lord's Supper? And the answer is, that if either of these ordinances be regarded as having anything to do with procuring salvation, then it falls into the same category of the rudiments of the world, which have been condemned and rejected. This includes, of course, all such theories as baptismal regeneration, transubstantiation and consubstantiation. If, however, these ordinances be regarded simply as figures and pledges, then their use does not come within the category referred to, but is of value to us in our spiritual life, even as God has so constituted all creation that His material works figure forth spiritual truth. But perhaps the question arises: May we multiply and elaborate ceremonies at our pleasure, provided only we do not regard them necessary to salvation? By no means, for a complicated and elaborate ceremonial, although free at the beginning from such perversion as this, necessarily though gradually dims the soul's direct view of Christ, and ends at length in an idolatry of observances. The believer's death with Christ has removed him out of the region of sensuous observances as interventions between God and himself, and brought him personally into direct and unhindered fellowship with God. He is already part and parcel of God's new creation. He *died from the world.*

Second. *We have in the text an argument based on this description of the Christian.* For example, in submitting himself to ordinances he practically contradicts his true citizenship, for such is the significance of the apostolic inquiry, "Why as though living in the world, do ye subject yourselves to ordinances?" **Really,** as we have seen, the Christian is not living in the world, but if he submits himself to such ordinances, he is acting as if he were in the world. In other words, he gives the lie to his profession as a Christian. His true citizenship is in the new creation, and if he appreciates it, he would not be dealing with the rudiments of the world. From this fact we learn that it is the Christian's duty and blessedness both to know and enjoy the actual experience of his heavenly citizenship.

But, furthermore, in submitting to the ordinances, the Christian is ascribing an inherent value of salvation to things which are fleeting and perishable, for such is the significance of the phrase in brackets, "Which things are all of them for destruction in the using up." The sense here is the same as in Matthew xv. 17, and the idea is that the things referred to could not be used without rendering them unfit for further use. Behold then the monstrous inconsistency of a Christian using these things as in any sense necessary to salvation, when he has already died with Christ from them, and become a part of the eternal new creation of God! Finally, it is useless for the Christian to submit himself to these ordinances, because they have no more than a mere show of wisdom. They have no real value in remedying indulgences of the flesh, or of eradicating evil. They are of the nature of will-worship, they are self-imposed ordinances, in other words, and make a show of great piety; but in the light of Christ's finished work for us, it is the very essence of unwisdom. Moreover, the humility associated therewith is only the garment of pride. Nor does a severe treatment of the body, however humble and disinterested it may seem, really extirpate the evil appetite of the flesh or the wicked passions of the soul. Starvation cannot do this, nor flagellation, nor dirt, nor squalor, nor any of these things.

26

THE TRUE ASCETICISM

"If then ye were raised together with Christ, seek the things above where Christ is, sitting on the right hand of God. Think the things above, not the things on the earth. For ye died, and your life has been hidden with Christ in God. When Christ, your life, shall be manifested, then shall ye also be manifested with Him in glory" (Col. iii. 1-4).

A T the close of the previous chapter the apostle had shown the believer to be dead with Christ from the rudiments of the world, and upon that he had based the argument that those believers who subjected themselves to ordinances violated their heavenly citizenship. They were ascribing an inherent value of salvation to things which were perishable, while they themselves were already partakers of the new Eternal creation. But now he follows this by showing the obligation and feasibleness of holy living enforced from this point of view. To be dead with Christ involves resurrection with Christ, and it is this last which avails against indulgence of the flesh.

First, *we have in this text a statement of the resurrection life of believers in Christ,* for when the apostle says, "If then, ye were raised together with Christ," he is stating not a problematical but a logical conclusion. It is, in other words, an absolute declaration of the fact that the believer has so risen. In the previous chapter he had asserted this, but now he re-asserts it as the result of dying with Christ. Dying with Christ and rising with Christ are as inseparable as the concave and the convex of a circle.

Notice the past tense in this case: "Ye were raised"; that is, it was an accomplished and completed fact for these Christians at Colossæ. Nor was it a mere ethical thing, a practical reformation, but a positive blessing, something confessed, LIFE, life by resurrection, life by resurrection together with Christ. His rising was our rising, His life our life. Thus are we brought face to face again with the truth concerning His perfect substitution for us and our perfect identification with Him. Remember that it is the same person who died who lives again; that is, we are not to conceive of the creation of a new person in the believer's case, but the creation by resurrection of a new life in the old person. If then, our resurrection with Christ is not a figure, but a real thing, it

shows inferentially that our death with Christ
is not a figure, but just as positive and just as
real. We speak of both, indeed, as judicial;
that is, a judicial faith and a judicial resurrection, but it is not the less real because of this.

Moreover, the apostle goes on to show that
our new life is Christ's own life in us, a fact
which is further demonstrated by the consideration that it is a hidden life. Hidden because Christ Himself is hidden. And when he
says that Christ Himself is our life he does
not mean merely that He is the author or giver
of our life, but that He Himself is the very
essence of it, just as in another place the same
apostle speaks of Him as our hope (I. Tim.
i. 1) and our peace (Eph. ii. 14). The illustration is that of the vine and the branches,
the head and the members of the body. (Compare here John xiv. 19, Gal. ii. 20, Eph. v. 30.)
Of course the text also shows that our Resurrection life in Christ is as well our Ascension
life and a life now seated with Him in heaven.
(Compare here Ephesians ii. 6.)

It is interesting to observe further, that our
life in Christ is a hidden life at the present
time. Our experience of it, for example, is
hidden in our own self-consciousness, so far as
the world is concerned, although this, perhaps,
is not the thought in the apostle's mind. The

meaning here is rather that our life is hidden in the heavens as Christ is hidden there in the bosom of God. It is concealed as far as its glory and highest characteristics are concerned, and also in the sense that it is there laid up in absolute and divine security. It is preserved there for further manifestation, and in that sense is an object of our faith. But when I say it is an object of our faith, I do not mean that we have no testimony to it at the present time in our own consciousness, which indeed, is true and precious, but only that it is an object of our faith so far as its grandest characteristics are concerned. And in this connection, notice the terms in which this hiddenness is described as furnishing an added intimation of its greatness and glory. It is said to be hidden with Christ in God! Not only is Christ our life, but He is our life in the bosom of God (John xvii. 21, 23; II. Peter i. 4).

Secondly. *We have in the text a statement of the obligation of the believer to realize his resurrection life in Christ,* to consider, and prize it, and appreciate it. "If then, ye were raised together with Christ, *seek the things above.*" For *"the things above"* examine such passages of Scripture as Matthew vi. 33, Gal. v. 26 and Phil. iii. 20. Here you will find the meaning to be such things as those where

Christ is at the right hand of God. Of course, when the apostle exhorts believers to "seek" the things above, he must not be understood to teach that these things are not theirs at the present time. The word "seek" means to search out and inquire into, ask for, examine. We are exhorted to seek them in this sense; in other words, to search them out as they are revealed to us in the holy Scriptures, and to be looking for and accepting them in our experience and possession.

And we are to *"think* the things above." Having sought them out or learned them, we are to *think* them in the sense that we are to keep our minds full of them. Habitual and positive thinking is meant. And meanwhile, we are *not* to think "the things on the earth." "The things on the earth" we are not to think of are ordinances, worldly power, wealth, ambition. We are not to think of them except in accordance with the standard of our resurrection life.

Thus what we are exhorted to is heavenly-mindedness, to have the mind full of, and to realize our Christ Life and all things above. This is the true asceticism. Now, such heavenly-mindedness is a holy power, for "as a man thinks, so he is." Such dying with Christ and living with Christ are in themselves both the ability and the spirit for overcoming evil and consecrating us to God. There is absolutely no other power for a holy life.

Thirdly. *We have in the text set before us the grand hope encouraging us to live this resurrection life.* So precious a life is in itself a perpetual impulse toward the realization of itself, for is it not in the nature of a treasure in possession to cause the owner to make much of it? Especially is this so when the treasure is a life.

But meanwhile it is a *hidden* treasure which must be appreciated by faith, toward the culture of which we need some special encouragement. And this we have in the grand hope that "When Christ shall be manifested, then shall we also be manifested with Him in glory." In other words, our Christ life is not always to be hidden, but is to come forth in full and glorious manifestation. Compare here, I. Peter i. 13, also Acts i. 11, I. Thess. iv. 16, II. Thess. i. 7-10. As Christ is one with us and we are one with Him, He could not die without us, nor rise without us, and now that He is our life He cannot come in glory without us. We shall come with Him (Rev. xix. 11-14). We shall be manifested in our coming with Him (Rom. viii. 19). We shall be manifested with Him in glory (John xvii. 22). Just what

Christ's glory will be is indicated in Matthew
xvii. 2, and Acts xxvi. 13, and His glory shall
be our glory (Matt. xiii. 43, Rev. iii. 21). All
of which is sure to come to pass, since He now
sits in kingly and judicial power (Ps. cx. 1).
Thus every way the power of holy living is
Heavenly-mindedness. What a cheery view of
a life consecrated to God!

In closing, let me ask you to examine I. John
iii. 1-3, for a paraphrase on our whole subject.

27

THE CONQUEST OF THE OLD NATURE

"Make dead then your members which are upon
the earth, fornication, uncleanness, lustfulness, evil
concupiscence and covetousness for as much as it is
idolatry. For such things' sake cometh the wrath of
God, in which things ye also walked once, when ye
were living in these things. But now do ye also
put off from you the whole:—anger, wrath, malice,
calumny, filthy abuse out of your mouth. Be not
lying one to another, putting off the old man with
his deeds and putting on the new; who is being renewed unto perfect knowledge according to the image
of Him that created him; where there is not Greek
and Jew, circumcision and uncircumcision, Barbarian, Scythian, bondman, and freeman, but Christ
is all things and in all things" (Col. iii. 5-11).

A T this point in the epistle the hortatory portion begins. The apostle has just concluded his argument by announcing the
grand principle of a holy life, and now he
seeks to apply that principle in ways of specific
exhortation. In the present instance those exhortations deal with the vices of the old man,

which, he tells us, can be conquered, and which a Christian is required to conquer.

First. *We have here an enumeration of those vices,* in verses 5 and 9. For example, he speaks of sins of impurity, of uncharitableness, and of insincerity. The sins of impurity include fornication, all uncleanness, lustfulness, which means any wicked or ungovernable affection, evil concupiscence, which is another name for evil desire or evil longings, and covet·ousness. Is it not remarkable that this last named vice should be classed with sins of uncleanness? And yet it is closely allied to them, for not only is selfishness the common foundation of it and them, but covetousness is selfishness procuring the means of indulgence in all uncleanness. Indeed, the apostle says *"the* covetousness," as though he would say, I speak of that which is the well-known servant of sins of sensual indulgence. He denominates this "idolatry," for which reason it is especially to be put off. Indeed, all sensual indulgences are idolatry, but covetousness preeminently so. "Ye cannot serve God and Mammon."

Under the head of sins of uncharitableness he includes anger, which represents a settled feeling, and wrath, which is the outburst of that feeling; malice, which represents a bent of mind for doing harm to others; calumny, and filthy abuse, the latter being still calumny, only of a filthy sort.

Under the head of sins of insincerity he speaks of lying, which, of course, is simply falsehood, cunning and deception. But it is noticeable that he refers to it in the present tense, "Be not lying," by which he means, let it not be true of you at any moment.

"For which things' sake cometh the wrath of God." The word "cometh" is in the present tense, as indicating that God's wrath is ever coming and never ceases to come forth against such things, affording a hint as to the watchfulness and enduring principles of God's moral government.

Second. *We have here a recognition of the new life of those whom the apostle is exhorting.* "In which things ye also walked once, when ye were living in those things." The idea is that they walked in those things as well as the other heathen people. Their life then was in the principle of these vices, and therefore their practice was full of them. But when he says "Ye were living in them," he implies necessarily that they were not living in them at the time when he speaks. A change had come over them, a new principle of life had taken hold of them, as we have seen in our preceding meditations. Now, as is the principle of life so is the living of the life. If these believers had not received this new life they would not have been in a position for him thus to exhort them to conquer evil. Instead of that he would have exhorted them to accept Christ and receive this new life, for only such can conquer evil. But such, let us remember, are required to do so.

We have, thirdly, to consider *the apostle's manner of exhorting*. A very important consideration indeed, as it will teach us how to battle with the evil in us and overcome it. He says, "Make dead your members which are upon the earth"; "put off from you the vices of the old man"; "putting off the old man with his deeds"; "putting on the new." These are his four formulas of exhortation. Let us consider them in their order.

(1) "Make dead your members which are upon the earth." In this instance we have the aorist imperative, which in the Greek indicates that the command is given in past time, and means that the thing needed is to be done by a single definite act and done completely. You are to make your members dead in a moment, and the act by which you make them so dead is a complete act. Now, since the believer has already died in Christ, as we have seen, to

make himself dead is simply to realize his death in Christ (Rom. vi. 11). He is to believe it, to think of it, and so to come into the power of it by the Holy Spirit. This is to practically "make dead," and it is done by a single definite completed act of realization. But, it may be asked: How does such realization give us power against the evil which is in us? The answer is, that it satisfies us as to the question of guilt; it satisfies our moral nature, and fills us with peace and joy which propels us towards a holy life with aversion from all our sins. If the soul moves thus freely from sin, that sin is conquered.

Notice especially that the apostle says make dead your *"members"*; that is, your hands or feet, or eyes, or ears, or tongue, or brain, "which are upon the earth." This is but another way of saying: Fill your soul with this realization and then your members will be governed accordingly. All your activities will be against your sins. At times your members may be in the seductive operation of temptation, but then it will be true of them that they are on the earth and not with Christ in the heavens, where they ought to remain. Now in the power of the Holy Spirit strike at once; make them dead; fill your soul with the realization of your death in and with Christ. In that

moment the evil spell is broken and you mount
upwards as on eagle's wings. This is the
great secret of the believer's power, not a re-
enacting of our death with Christ, but a realization of it. We are never exhorted to crucify
ourselves with Christ. That has been already
done, and since Christ died once for all it
never can be redone. Our duty is to realize the
death already accomplished, and so ourselves
become practically dead. Let it not be said
that this cannot be done while we are yet in
the midst of the active evil of our old nature,
for since the apostle commands it, *God* commands it, and through the Holy Spirit will
help it to be accomplished if we will.

(2) "Put off from you" the sins of the old
man. Having made dead your members which
are on the earth, the sins of your members are
put off from you at once. The putting off is
effected by the making dead. It is a real suc-
cess. Here again the aorist imperative is used,
and the "putting off" is shown to be a single
definite act which is completely done, rather
than a gradual experience. We gain strength
of realization as we cultivate it, but at any
moment the act of realization is the putting off
from us of our sins.

(3) "Putting off the old man with his
deeds." Put off from you, not only the sins

of the old man but the old man himself. Make dead not only that part of the sinful self consisting of the members of the body, but the whole of the sinful self. Realize that in your death with Christ the whole of your standing with the first Adam was destroyed, and that you have died from your original condition of being (Rom. viii. 9). You are now in the second Adam and invested with all his beauty and fragrance. What a mighty power such a realization is!

(4) "Putting on the new" man. Realize that from your death with Christ has resulted a new life; that out of the destruction of your old man has arisen a new man, a living entity, the image of God, your childhood to God. You can now think, and feel, and enjoy in the power of a heavenly nature. You can run the race set before you. With regard to this new man, the apostle adds, "who is being renewed unto perfect knowledge, according to the image of Him who created him." This means that the new man grows stronger and stronger every day in a continuous, ever advancing process. It is *"unto perfect knowledge,"* a knowledge not alone of the intellect but of the heart; a knowledge which includes faith and experience as well; moral and spiritual knowledge, which is power. Every item of true knowledge

gained is growth and the conquest of evil.
Meanwhile, in thus being renewed "unto perfect knowledge" the new man is being con-
formed more and more to the image of Him
that created him; not merely that image of God
in which Adam was made and which he partly
lost, but something higher, richer and more
glorious than that, even the image of Him who
created the *new* man.   In this latter creation
God did a nobler work than the former (Rom.
viii. 29).   As we thus grow in the knowledge
of God, we grow to be like God.   To know
God is to think as God thinks, and feel as God
feels, and be brought into His image in that
sense.   How mighty the realization of this act
is to the overthrow of the stronghold of Satan
and sin!

Moreover, in this new man "there is not
Greek and Jew, circumcision and uncircumcision, barbarian, scythian, bondman, freeman,
but Christ is all things and in all things."   The
new man is not depending on such distinctions,
since he did not come from them and is not
nourished by them.   No one has received the
new nature because he is a Greek or Jew, because he is a Barbarian or Scythian (the worst
of barbarians), or because he is a slave or
freeman, for these are worldly distinctions and
they disappear in Christ.   One may receive the

new nature and become a new man although he be a Greek or Jew, a Barbarian or a Scythian, a bondman or a freeman, for "Christ is all things." He has obliterated all such distinctions, substituting Himself for them and making nothing but Himself answer for pardon and purity. His own death, His own blood, His own resurrection are the sole means, the all-sufficient means of saving the soul. What a mighty power as against evil is an appreciation of this independence of the new man with reference to all worldly distinctions! and what a prevention it is of all waste of time and efforts, since it shuts up the soul simply and directly to Christ. These distinctions may concern our responsibility of service, but not in any sense our salvation or our power against evil. Christ Himself is our strength and our victory.

28

THE TRIUMPH OF THE NEW NATURE

"Clothe yourselves, then, as elect ones of God, holy and having been beloved, with bowels of compassion, kindness, humbleness of mind, meekness, long-suffering (forbearing one another and forgiving each other if any have a complaint against any, as even the Lord forgave ye, so also ye). But over all these, Love, which thing is the bond of perfectness. And let the peace of Christ rule in your hearts, to which ye were also called in one body. And be ye thankful" (Col. iii. 12-15).

BEFORE beginning the exposition of these verses, let me call attention to the use of the tenses, past and present; for it may interest some to know that with Paul actual exhibitions of life and character on the part of the Christian are usually, if not always, expressed in the present tense, while the principles on which such exhibitions depend are expressed in the past tense. Indeed, this distinction in the uses of the tenses is a kind of epitome of all that the Gospel teaches us on the subject of holy living.

To come now to the connection between the present theme and the preceding one, it were perhaps enough to say that the specific exhortations begun in that are continued in this. There they refer to the putting off of the vices of the old nature, while here to the putting on of the graces of the new nature.

First, let us consider the graces of the new nature, or the new man, as here indicated. There are at least nine of them:

(1) *Bowels of Compassion.* That is, deep, earnest, yearning, genuine compassion, a heart of compassion, of interest, deep fellow-feeling.

(2) *Kindness.* That is, benevolence, sweetness of intercourse, involving beneficence.

(3) *Humbleness of Mind.* That is, the moral habit from which the two preceding graces spring, since self-conceit, pride, or arrogance can never produce them. Nor can mere natural temperament sufficiently supply and sustain them. Only a true sense of our own ill-desert before God is the fountain of hearty compassion and sustained kindness toward the miserable. It is as we think and feel in a lowly manner of ourselves that we think and feel according to what is the truth.

(4) *Meekness,* which is one of the effects of humility and has reference primarily to our relations with God. (See James i. 21.) But

this submissiveness toward God immediately
operates in all our relations towards men, for
it means that submission to God in the trials
which come to us in His providence from men.
(See II. Sam. xvi. 11.)   It is opposed to rude-
ness and harshness.

(5) *Long-suffering,* which is merely another expression for the full operation of meekness, especially as opposed to resentment,
wrath or revenge.

(6) *Forbearing and Forgiving,* two words
which explain the operation of meekness and
long-suffering.   Forbearing to be impatient
and to avenge one's self, and, on the contrary,
to be forgiving.   And this whenever we have
a complaint.   The formal act of forgiveness,
indeed, cannot be performed without repentance and confession on the part of the of-
fender; but in the absence of such repentance
and confession the spirit of forgiveness should
be within our hearts in the fulness of its power.
We should essentially forgive even though the
formal forgiveness cannot be pronounced. And
the powerful motive for this is that the Lord
forgave us.

(7) *Love.* This grace is to put on over all
the others as a kind of outer garment, or, more
properly, to use the figure of the apostle, as
"the bond of perfectness," that is, the bond

which holds together all the graces of perfection, which embraces them as is seen in I. Corinthians xiii. 4-7. Without it they are all delusive; compassion is only sentiment, humility is debasement, and meekness is cajolery and deceit without love.

(8) *Peace;* and notice that this is the peace of Christ (John xiv. 27; Eph. ii. xiv). It is indeed the same as the peace of God (Phil. iv. 7), only there it is opposed to anxious worldliness, while here to the hard and unloving spirit. The peace of Christ is not merely a judicial fact such as that peace with God referred to in Romans v. i, but a kind of feeling which we are to possess and exhibit towards others. And this peace is inseparable from love, for our love is the result of our sense of God's love. The peace, in other words, that fills us with serenity and tranquility in all our relations with men. To this peace we were called when we were forgiven of God, and we were called to it in one Body, which means that mystical Body composed of all true believers, of which Christ is Himself the Head, and concerning which we have already treated in preceding chapters. In the present instance the idea is that in the operations of this peace we are to realize the unity of the Body of Christ. We are to let it rule in our hearts,

and the word "rule" means to preside there as
an umpire in the games to decide and award
the prizes. Peace is the one supreme umpire,
the one absolute referee in difficulties. In the
conflict of motives, or impulses, or reasons, the
feeling of peace with God steps in to decide,
and in that case feeling is power.

(9) *"And be ye thankful."* True thankfulness is the essence of Christian experience and
enjoyment; it is the appreciation of our own
new life and the very spirit of Christian power.

Secondly, let us consider the exhortation to
put on these graces.

(1) We are exhorted to "clothe" ourselves
with them, or, in other words, to clothe ourselves with the new man or the new nature,
for the graces of the new man we cannot have
except as we have the new man himself. Just
as we cannot put off the deeds of the old man
except as we put off the old man himself, so we
cannot put on the graces of the new man except
as we have put on the new man himself. Of
course, those whom the apostle is exhorting
already possessed the new man, as we have
seen, and none others could possibly put on the
graces. But how, it may be asked, are they to
clothe themselves with that which they have
already put on? The idea is that they are to
realize that they have it on. They are to real-

ize their dying with Christ and their rising
with Christ, that is, understand it, believe it,
think it, and so by the power of the Holy
Spirit come under the influence of it. Now, if
the new man be thus felt and appreciated, he
must put forth his activities, the graces will
show themselves; in other words, just as flowers bloom on a vigorous tree. And this realization of our dying and rising with Christ is a
single, definite act, a realization of something
done once for all. It is the aorist imperative
we have in the words "Clothe yourselves."
You distinctly think that you died and rose
with Christ, and that it has been done completely and forever, which is the only way to
realize your possession in Christ. At the same
time this one distinct act of realization is then
to be repeated continually. It may be illustrated by ownership of worldly property. By a
definite act of thought the owner realizes the
fact of his right to that property and that his
right was a perfectly established thing of the
past, yet as often as necessary he repeats the
act of realization.

(2) At the same time, while realizing the
new man and thus providing for the being
clothed with the graces, we are also to realize
distinctly the necessity and importance of each
particular grace as belonging to and befitting

the new man. This will bring one under the power of each activity of the new man.

(3) Our realizations of all these should be based upon the ground of our being "elect ones of God, holy and having been beloved," which is only to say that our realization of the new man should measure up to the full realization of the subject. We are "elected ones of God" in the sense that God's election of us preceded the judicial facts of our dying and rising with Christ, and proves that His infinite heart was set upon us (Ephesians i. 4). Of course we cannot realize this except as we know it for a fact, which is in itself something very precious and powerful toward a holy life.

Now, as *"elected ones of God"* we are holy, that is, we are sainted and set apart for God, (1) by the act of election, (2) by the judicial act of our dying with Christ, (3) by the act of our rising with him, (4) by our association with Him, and (5) by the Holy Spirit's developing within us all these judicial facts in regard to us into one conscious fact and power.

Finally, as "elect ones of God" we *"have been beloved."* We *were* beloved or else we had never been elect ones, and, once beloved, we are still beloved. God did love us and loves us now. Our election and our sanctification both prove it. And now we love Him because He first loved us, and love is the bond of all the graces.

Such are our good works, and such is the way to perform them.

29

THE MEANS OF POWER

"Let the word of Christ dwell in you richly in all wisdom; teaching and admonishing each other in psalms, hymns, spiritual songs in grace, singing in your hearts to God. And everything, whatsoever ye do in word or in deed, all things do in the name of the Lord Jesus, giving thanks to God the Father through Him" (Col. iii. 16, 17).

IT may be interesting to call attention to the fact that none but present tenses are used in this passage, since it was remarked in the previous chapter that when the exhortation concerns the principle and power of holy living, it is put in the past tense as directing us to the accomplished work of Christ; but when it has reference to our use of means, as the study of the word for example, or to our actual manifestation of the graces of the Christian life it is put in the present tense.

The connections of our text in this case are very important. In the first four verses of the chapter, the apostle taught us the principle and power of all holy living by showing us that as believers we have life out of death with

Christ, life in the rising with Christ, etc.; then, in verses 5 to 11, he appplied this power to the putting off of the vices of our old sinful nature, teaching us to use the facts of our death and resurrection with Christ for that purpose; and in verses 12 to 15 He made the same application with regard to the putting on of the graces of the new man, teaching us to use the same facts in the same way. The whole emphasis of all these exhortations is on the facts of our past death and resurrection with Christ. But now, to insure our use of this principle and power of holy living he adds the first verse of this text: "Let the word of Christ dwell in you richly in all wisdom," etc. Study the Scriptures, get your ideas of Christ from them, keep your soul full of them, is the thought he would set before us in these words. He had previously indicated the same truth, but now he is more explicit. Acquaintance with and realization of the scriptural ideas of Christ will insure both the truthfulness and thoroughness of service to God.

And as regards the second verse of the text, "And everything, whatsoever ye do," etc., he seems to sum up universal obedience to God in the one thing of always acting in the name of the Lord Jesus. Everywhere, and at every instant this is the one principle and power of victory over evil, and of progress in holiness.

In the two verses of our text then, we have two exhortations each one co-extensive with its verse. But each of the two may be distributed again into various parts. The first has three parts. The "indwelling of the word," "teaching and admonishing," "singing in the heart to God." Or, to express it in another form, it is first, the indwelling of the word; secondly, the outgoing of the word; and thirdly, the indwelling again.

First—Under the head of the first exhortation let us consider the indwelling—*"Let the word of Christ dwell in you richly in all wisdom."* "The word of Christ" might mean either the word spoken by Christ or the word which exhibits Christ. In fact, however, these two interpretations come to the same thing, since every word spoken by Christ had for its design the exhibition of Himself. The meaning here is doubtless, that of the exhibiting of Christ in the word. This would seem to be necessitated by the larger context and the additional fact that "the word of Christ" is a phrase nowhere else found in the Bible. Why, then, this unique phraseology, unless it be for the reason that, in accordance with his general course he would here call emphatic attention to the word as setting forth, in Christ's death and resurrection, and in His identification with us, the principle and power of holy living?

Observe that we are to let the word of Christ dwell in us, not among us, but in us. We are not merely to have the truth taught to us, in articles of faith and creeds, but to have it in us as a present experience (Romans 8:11, II Timothy 1:5, 13). It should be in us as *dwelling* there, inhabiting us as its house and home. It should not be treated as a stranger, or slave at a distance, but received as an everyday and intimate guest, rather indeed, as the master of the house who regulates all things in it. It should dwell in us *richly,* that is, plentifully, in all its principles, and all its various modes of expression in the scripture. It should dwell in us richly in the sense that we should treasure it in all appreciation of its excellences. It should dwell in us *in all wisdom. Wisdom* is the knowledge of the best means to the best end. The word of Christ is in us "in all wisdom" when we see and appreciate the necessary connection between the believer's position in Christ and holy living. As this exhortation is addressed to all Christians, let us apply it to ourselves.

Under the head of the first exhortation, let us next consider the *outgoing* of the word of Christ. Although a dweller at home, it is to

go forth in various visitations, teaching, for
example, and admonishing, which means the
application of the truth in rebuke and warning. This teaching and admonishing are to
be in *"psalms, hymns and spiritual songs."*
The "psalm" was a song accompanied by in-
instrumental music, from the word *psallo,* to
touch; the "hymn" was a song of praise to
God; and what is here called a "song" (Greek,
ode,) was the general name for a song of
whatever kind, whether accompanied or unac-
companied, and on whatever subject.
"Psalms" therefore seems to refer specifically
to the songs of David; "hymns" to songs of
praise composed by Christians; "odes" to all
forms of song with no limitation except that
they shall be spiritual. Now, the apostle does
not mention these various songs as referring
necessarily to public services, but they were
thus to teach and admonish each other at their
various gatherings, that is, their family gatherings, social gatherings, etc. It was to be a
daily, life-long service of song, but always as
teaching and admonishing. Instruction and
warning as thus conveyed would be uttered in
strong and pleasant feelings, and also with the
force which the charm of sweet songs might
impart. But observe particularly that the singing was to be *"in grace,"* not in gracefulness

necessarily, not as well done artistically, but in *the* grace which is from God in the heart, the gracious power of the Holy Spirit there accompanying the dwelling of the word of Christ in the soul. Sing your instructions and warnings to each other as you yourself feel and enjoy the truth.

Finally, in this connection let us consider the *indwelling again.* The word of Christ while going forth on its mission ever comes back again to its house and home. *"Singing in your hearts to God,"* says the apostle: This refers to such singing as may be involved in the soul's personal intercourse with God. It is, therefore, private singing such as may be when one is alone with God. It is singing "in the heart," in the thoughts. The scriptural ideas of Christ fill us with joy, and peace, and holy consecration and make our very thoughts as notes of music to God. Was ever anything more beautiful? Here is assurance and here is blessedness. And it is very noticeable that after speaking of our teaching and admonishing others, the apostle turns his thoughts to the indwelling of the word in our own soul. He thus guards against the danger ever threatening, that we shall feed others while yet we may starve ourselves. While watering we should also be watered. And yet there is always the danger of the opposite being true of us unless thus we are upon our guard.

Secondly.   In speaking now of the second exhortation let us observe that it has two parts.

(1.)   The doing of everything *"in the name of the Lord Jesus."*   The name of a man is that which distinguishes, identifies, sums him up and the name of Christ is all that Christ is as man, as God, and as the God-man for the purpose of His substitutionary death for us sinners.   Any idea of Him short of this is a failure to name Him.   *Doing* in His name is to act in the realization of Him under these precise and distinctive ideas.   It is to do a thing as knowing Him who has accomplished His work for us as His expiatory sacrifice and righteousness; it is to know ourselves to have been in Him when He died and to have died and risen with Him.   Therefore it is to do a thing in the joy of realized salvation, and of realized oneness with Him and in the felt power of fellowship with Him.   This is the one principle and power of all acceptable service.

(2.)   But we are to do this *" giving thanks to God the Father through Him."*   This is said to mark the fact that any effective naming of Christ is with the heart and in the power of realization.   This means joyous, loving, obliging thoughts—thoughts of God's love sent up to God through Christ, Who is the one channel from God to us and from us to God. So let us be consecrated to God.

30

THE EXHIBITION OF POWER

"Wives, submit yourselves unto your husbands, as it is fit in the Lord. Husbands, love your wives, and be not bitter against them. Children, obey your parents in all things; for this is well-pleasing in the Lord. Fathers, provoke not your children, else they be disheartened. Bond-servants, obey in all things your masters according to the flesh; not with acts of eye-service as men-pleasers, but in singleness of heart, fearing the Lord. Whatever ye do, do it diligently from the heart, as to the Lord and not to men; knowing that of the Lord ye shall receive the recompense of the inheritance; ye serve the Lord Christ. For he that doeth wrong shall receive back that which he did wrongfully; and there is no respect of persons. Masters, give on your part to your bond-servants justice and fairness; knowing that ye also have a Master in heaven" (Col. iii. 18-iv. 1).

WE have now before us certain special exhortations with regard to the duties of our social relations, in which we have an opportunity to exhibit the spiritual power of holy living, the means of which was considered in the preceding lecture. Three great instances are here selected: wives and husbands; children and parents; slaves and masters. These

exhortations are in a sense subordinate to the
general ones previously considered, and are in
the nature of an application of them in certain
instances. Those indeed include these, for if
the vices of the old man be put off and the
graces of the new man be put on, all and each
of the duties of our social relations cannot but
be properly attended to. But the apostle
wishes to be very explicit since he is exceedingly urgent on the subject of holy living. He
is not content with his exhortations against our
sins, and on behalf of the graces of our new
life, but makes special applications with reference to particular relations.

First. *As to wives and husbands.* In the
wife's submission to her husband, as thus enforced by reference to her position in Christ,
and in the husband's application of love and
gentleness to his wife there is involved the
sacredness of marriage. The wife's submission is positively commanded, and is not affected by the reference in Galatians, 3:28, to
the effect that "There is neither male nor female in Jesus Christ." "Male and female are
one" as regards salvation in Christ, but that
does not contravene the Creator's established
relations of life. But in this submission there
is nothing derogatory to the woman, since sub-
ordination and order are the great character-

istics of God's workmanship. Compare here
first Corinthians, 11 :3, and Ephesians 5 :22-33.
In these places the apostle associates the
wife's submission to her husband with Christ's
submission to God. As there is nothing derogatory to Christ in his submission so there is
nothing derogatory to the woman in her submission.   It is no "robbery" of God that
Christ is equal to God, and yet the Son is submissive to the Father ; so it is no robbery to the
husband that the wife is equal to him, and she
is his equal though her sphere be different, and
yet she is submissive to him. The question of
woman's position and duties is not of modern
origin, since it was agitated in the apostle's
own day among the women of the Church at
Corinth, and so far as the modern relation is
concerned that question is here authoritative-
ly settled. It is " fit in the Lord." That means
fit in Christ that the wife should submit to her
husband. The reference is, of course, to the
believing wife, she who is "in Christ," a saved
woman, having a vital oneness with Him as
the branch is one with the vine. The reference
is to the woman who so appreciates her standing in Christ as to be able to feel the fitness of
things resulting therefrom. She practices her
submission to her husband in the sweetness and
completeness of her relations to Christ.

Passing from the consideration of the wife's submission to the husband's love, we cannot but notice that the apostle does not say husbands *command* your wives. And why does he not so say, since it is correlative to the word "submit"? This is very significant. While the duty of submission is enforced on the one side, the prerogative of commanding is not enforced on the other side. He does not deny that prerogative, but neither does he so much as mention it. It is not his purpose to enforce prerogatives, since they need no enforcement. Neither is it his purpose to exalt and magnify the husband over his wife. He recognizes his authority, but does not say one word which might have the effect to exaggerate the husband in his own estimation with reference to his wife. But he does say, "Husbands love your wives." This love includes every attention, honor, service and delight in her society, every deference to her wishes and the reposing of his confidence in her, as well as the enjoyment of his oneness with her in Christ. What more is it possible for the wife to desire? Thus if the husband be fixed in his place of authority, is not the wife exalted to stand by his side? Moreover, it is added, "be not bitter" against your wife. Here the husband is specifically warned against tyranny on the ground of his authority. In all his relations with his wife love must rule. There is no place here for bad tempers, or impatience, or lack of considerateness or any selfishness.

Second. *As to children and parents.* In the first place children are to *obey,* and this *"in all things."* This is the rule, though exceptions are easy to be understood. The rule as thus expressed, however, is proof of the importance attached to the principle of the child's obedience. The grounds on which the child is to render this obedience is the most exalted in character, for he is thus to act because it it *"well-pleasing in the Lord."* By the Lord here is meant Christ, and as the *"well-pleasing"* is said to be *in* Christ, rather than *to* Christ, the meaning must be that such children as are in Christ will render obedience to their parents in the very love and joy of their position in Him. Obedience is well-pleasing to them, because they are in Christ.

But, furthermore, *fathers must not provoke their children,* which includes mothers, as well, no doubt. To "provoke not" means to be not unduly severe; the child's obedience is to be required, the proper discipline is to be exercised, but the family government is to be tempered, qualified, and in a sense glorified by parental love in Christ. Otherwise the child may become *"disheartened,"* desperate, and an easy prey to the wicked influences which are ever at work around him.

Third. *As to slaves and masters.* Slaves must obey their "masters according to the flesh in all things," necessary exceptions being, as in the other cases, easily understood. They are not to serve with *eye-service,* as men-pleasers, but in singleness of heart. This means undividedness of heart, without dishonesty, duplicity, or false show of industry, and at the same time to be *"fearing the Lord."* That is, doing everything diligently and from the heart as though it were being done to Christ Himself, rather than to man. And the slave's encouragement in this obedience is the fact that of Christ he shall receive *"the recompense of the inheritance."* Notice that the word "recompense" is modified by the word "inheritance," teaching that it is not a recompense of *merit* which the faithful slave or servant received, since it is an inheritance which constitutes the recompense. Nevertheless, it is a recompense and a most blessed compensation. In Matthew xxi. 35-38, the servant and the heir are contrasted, but here they are one and the same; for this believer in Christ, though he be the slave of man, is at the same time, the free man of Christ, and as a son of God he is a joint heir with Christ. And he *knows* that it is so. He cannot fail of the recompense for he *serves the Lord Christ* who never disappoints His servants, therefore let him do all his obedience faithfully. And to stir him further to this faithfulness, he is warned that *"he that doeth wrong shall receive back that which he did wrongfully."* That is, he may expect retribution proportioned to his offense. But indeed this warning applies to both master and slave, and to any and everyone, for, as the text reads: *"There is no respect of persons,"* neither of the slave nor the master. Compare here Leviticus xix. 15.

And then there are obligations for the masters which, on their part, are as imperative as those pertaining to the servants. They must give to their bond-servants justice and fairness, for they also *"have a Master in Heaven."* He that doeth wrong shall receive back that which he did wrongfully, even though he be a master.

In the conclusion of this section of our epistle, there are two or three general reflections which suggest themselves. For example, in each of the three relationships, the apostle begins with the duties of the inferior or subjected party, an arrangement which is not accidental, as we may judge by comparing Ephesians v. 22

and the subsequent verses, as well as I. Peter
2:18 and the subsequent verses. One reason
for this may be that the duties of submission
and obedience are so incomparably important
to all the interests of human life. A further
reflection is suggested by the fact that so
large a space is given to the relationship of
slaves and masters, as compared with that allotted to each of the other two, the same pecu-
liarity being seen in the passages in Ephesians
and Peter just referred to. The reason of this
may be that slavery is not the intuitively sacred relation which either of the others is, thus
making the obedience of the slave peculiarly
hard and repulsive. The apostle needs, therefore, to be more explicit and urgent. The principles of the Gospel must always lead to the
abolition of slavery, but wherever it exists it
involves obedience. Finally, all these duties
of our social relations are here seen in special
connection with the believer's standing in
Christ. His Deity is brought out since it is
Him we fear, Him we serve, and to Him we
direct all our actions. It is He, moreover, who
dispenses the recompense of the inheritance, or
inflicts the final punishment. But not only is
His Deity emphasized, but also the salvation
which is in Him, and which is brought to bear
on our discharge of duty. It is as we are in

Him that we render our obedience to God, a circumstance which connects the whole of this practical obligation with the whole of the preceding portion of the chapter. Salvation is the fountain of obedience, and the present Christ is our strength and victory.

31

THE SECRET OF POWER

"Continue steadfast in prayer, being awake therein in thanksgiving. Withal praying also for us, that God may open unto us a door of the word, to speak the mystery of Christ, on account of which I have been also in bonds; that I may make it manifest, as I ought to speak. Walk in wisdom towards them that are without, buying up for yourselves the opportunity. Let your speech be always in grace, having been seasoned with salt, so that ye have known how ye ought to answer every one" (iv. 2-6).

THIS passage contains certain specific exhortations which may be distributed into two general divisions: those concerning Prayer, and those concerning our Behaviour or Conduct in the world.

I. Let us consider the exhortation concerning prayer which is included in verses 2 to 4. And to begin with, notice how aptly the subject of prayer is here introduced. We have been exhorted to put off the vices of the old man, to put on the graces of the new man, to study the word of Christ, to teach that word in the joy of our own experience of it, to do all these things in the name of the Lord Jesus, giving

thanks to God through Him, and to exemplify
the graces of the new man in our various relations to one another; moreover, we have been
exhorted to do all these things in the power of
the realization of our oneness with Christ in
death and in resurrection. Thus the entire
operation of practical holiness has been opened
up before us. But to know how to proceed is
one thing, while the strength to do it is another
thing. We need the Holy Spirit; we need His
gift of heart appreciation, and all His gracious
workings in us in order to that end. This is
the secret of the Christian's power from the
Divine side. Christ, indeed, is Himself our
Strength as well as our Way; but the Spirit of
God must enable us to apprehend Christ in the
fulness of the blessing of the gospel of peace.
Hence we should pray for the Holy Spirit; for
God has promised to give Him to them that
ask Him. Without prayer we can do nothing.

And yet, what is prayer good for except as it
is associated with the heart's action in the faith
of Christ? If we do not take hold of Christ,
and receive Him in confidence, how possibly
shall the Holy Spirit strengthen us, for He
strengthens us only with Christ? If we do not
search into the things of Christ, and meditate
on them, how can we reasonably expect the
Holy Spirit for whom we are asking? If we

do not labor for clearness and definite views of our dying with Christ and rising again with Him, then we are ignoring the very elements of joy and peace which the Holy Spirit has spread before us in His own written word. How then, can we ask Him for the strength of joy and peace in the work of holy living, while we are at the same time indifferent about the ground-work of it as already given us in these, His inspired words? Thus it is that the subject of prayer comes in here at the close of these exhortations. In this arrangement itself a great lesson is taught in prayer. We are depending on the imparted power of the Holy Spirit, and we must pray to have that power; but we, ourselves, must understand the truth and believe it.

Following this introduction, let us notice that we are exhorted to *pray for ourselves,* since such is the meaning of the apostle's words in verse two, when compared with verse 3. Prayer for ourselves, while keeping in view God's providential blessings, mainly is concerned with the Holy Spirit's help to enable us to apprehend Christ more and more fully, to realize our risen life in Him, and thus, in the power of clear convictions and conscious blessedness, to live a holy life. The faith based upon these convictions, which is so essential to

true prayer, we cannot have except as it comes
to us through the gift of the Holy Spirit;
nevertheless we are to believe, to search, to
meditate, to accept and to appropriate the
truth, and in that way cultivate faith so far as
it is within the range of our ability to do so.
Then, notice that we must continue *steadfast in
prayer.* That is, there must be perseverance,
acquiescence in God, constancy in our exercises, as illustrated in Luke xviii, 1-8; Acts i.
14; Romans. xii. But in order to have this
steadfast continuance we need to be *awake*
in prayer both in mind and heart. Otherwise there will be wanderings, and
distraction of thought, and a listless
frame of mind and faithlessness. We
need to be awake *before* we pray, that we may
be awake *while* we pray, that our attention
flag not, that our humility before God fail not,
that our fervor decay not, that our confidence
linger not. And we need to be awake *after*
prayer, that we may act consistently with our
petitions, that we may look for answers to
them and yet wait God's time for answering
them. And if it be asked, How shall we secure
this wakefulness? The answer is, by culti-
vating the spirit and exercises of thanksgiving.
"Being awake therein in thanksgiving." Joy
is always awake. Gladness ever keeps its eyes

open. But the feeling of discouragement is drowsy. Hopeless care causes listlessness and slavish duty falls asleep. To have the spirit of faith, to receive Christ in the fulness of His salvation, to appropriate Him is peace, joy, conscious blessedness, thankfulness. And such thankfulness is always wide awake.

But furthermore, this prayer is not only for ourselves but also for the extension of the Gospel among men. See verses 3 and 4. *"Withal praying also for us,"* that is, for me, Paul, and my associates, Timothy, Epaphras, and the others. Pray *"that God may open to us a door of the word."* The "word" here means the Gospel, the request being that all obstructions may be taken out of the way of it as it shall be delivered by the preacher. Ask God to make men willing to hear, and not to shut off the Word from themselves by their ignorance and pride. Particularly would He have them pray for liberty *"to speak the mystery of Christ,"* the meaning of which has been already explained in part in the previous chapters. He wishes liberty to proclaim the equal privileges of Gentile and Jew in the Kingdom of God. Had Paul been content to preach a Judaic gospel he might have been still at large instead of being a prisoner in bonds (Acts xxi. 28; xxii. 21, 22). He wishes to make this mystery manifest as he "ought to speak." This shows his disinterestedness, and that he has no thought of his own personal discomfort in the prison, but only that he might be set at liberty therefrom for the Gospel's sake. That expression *"as I ought to speak"* means so much. It speaks of the thoughtfulness, the accuracy, the fulness of statement with which he desired to manifest this mystery because of his sense of its preciousness. It was no light matter to Paul that he had been made a preacher of the Gospel, hence he so often asks for the prayers of the people.

Secondly, having considered the division concerning prayer, let us now consider that concerning our Behavior and Conduct. This concerns *"them that are without,"* that is, those who are outside of the brotherhood or family of Christ. These are the unconverted, as indicated in I. Corinthians v. 12, 13 and I. Thessalonians iv. 12. Towards these we are to *"walk in wisdom"* and to let our *"speech be alway in grace."* All the previous exhortations of the apostle have related to the personal Gospel culture of Christians themselves, and to their intercourse among themselves; but now, having concluded these exhortations, he speaks of the duty of the Christian towards "them that are without." This is in accordance with the dis-

tinction observed in other scriptures, as, for
instance, Galatians vi. 10; I. Thessalonians iii.
12; II. Peter i. 7, etc. In the last named instance, "brotherly kindness" and "charity" are
spoken of, the first referring to love to the
brotherhood of Christ, and the second to love
to others generally. The brotherhood of Christ
is a world in itself, having its own life, its own
peculiar interests, and its own work. But at
the same time we have duties towards those
who are outside of it; the honor of the Gospel
in their eyes is intrusted to our keeping, and it
is our commission to win from them additions
to our own number. These duties we discharge
just in the measure in which we observe those
exhortations which relate to our own external
life as members of the brotherhood of Christ.

Our first duty is to *"walk in wisdom"* towards the unconverted. Wisdom is Gospel
knowledge applied in Gospel common sense. It
includes the uprightness of the Christian's daily
life, and consistency with his profession. It includes also the distinctiveness of the Christian's life as self-exhibited. We cannot hope
either to honor the truth in the eyes of the
unconverted or to win them to Christ, except
as we show forth the essential difference of the
Christian's position from that of the world.
And yet, in setting this forth there must be no

seeking for stage effect, no self-conceit and no
mere oddities. The truth as it is in Jesus, that
is, the distinctive teachings of the Gospel must
have become so inwrought into our personal
consciousness as to come forth into view with
spontaneity and ease, and the freshness of life,
whether in our conversation or in our separation from certain worldly engagements. But
"walk in wisdom" includes still more, namely,
the conscious blessedness of the life of the
Christian as a visible fact. It is anything but
wisdom towards "them that are without" for
the Christian to manifest a life without joy,
or peace, or comfort, since such a life is a practical denial to them of the blessedness of the
Gospel. Even amid afflictions "the joy of the
Lord" should be our strength. This includes
finally, a sanctified humanity of feeling towards
"them that are without"; that is, sympathy
with all genuine human interests, such as the
proprieties and amenities of social intercourse;
a loving concern, earnest yet respectfully
shown for the salvation of souls. Now in all
these ways, in order to behave ourselves wisely
in the world it is necessary that we be "buying
up for ourselves the opportunity." Circumstances are ever changing, and to know just
when to speak and how to speak, when to act
and how to act, to know just how to use oppor-

tunity, how to keep ourselves in fullest appreciation of the truth and in sincere sympathy with human interests—this is wisdom. This requires effort, thought, watchfulness, freshness, and this is what is meant by "buying the opportunity." But we are not only to "walk in wisdom toward them that are without," but also to have *our speech alway in grace* toward them. (See James iii.) Furthermore, in order to have our speech always in grace it must have been *"seasoned with salt."* What is this seasoning with salt? Since salt gives flavor and relish to our food, so whatever gives adaptation and point to our speech is that which seasons it. The ancients spoke much of the salt of human speech, and "Attic salt" has become a kind of proverb. This means wit, but the inspired apostle is not referring to wit, but simply to that suitableness of discourse which, in the very nature of the case, is associated with the milk of wisdom—"words fitly spoken." Such speech is gracious or acceptable to them that are without, even though they may not be convinced by it or in any way essentially affected. Thus speaking we shall show them we know how to answer everyone. Our answers may not suffice to satisfy the objections presented to us, but they will be the proper answers for us to have given.

Here ends the hortatory division of our
epistle, and what an exhibition of practical
holiness it presents! How wide the field, how
searching the duties, and yet how repeatedly
and urgently it is taught that the foundation
principle of the whole is our own personal
realization of the salvation which is in Christ!

32

PERSONAL GREETINGS

WE have now reached the fourth and final division of the epistle with its Personal Greetings, the gentle sweetnesses of Christian intercourse thus crowning and gilding both the sublimity, and the doctrine and the works of holy living. The division includes the twelve final verses of the apostle, and may be distributed in four parts: Those which concern the bearers of the epistle, those which contain greetings from brethren, those which are the apostle's salutations to special friends, and his autographic salutation to the whole Church.

First, let us consider the verses which concern the bearers of the epistle, 7-9, which read as follows:

"All my state shall Tychicus declare unto you, the beloved brother, and faithful minister and fellow-servant in the Lord; whom I sent unto you for the same purpose, that ye might know of our estate, and that he might comfort your hearts; with Onesimus, the faithful and beloved brother, who is among you. They shall make known unto you all things here."

Tychicus and Onesimus were sent together,
and were bearers of the epistle. For further
allusions to the first-named see Acts xx. 4;
Ephesians vi. 21; II. Timothy iv. 12, and Titus
iii. 12. He is called *"the beloved brother";*
that is, a Christian dear to the apostle's heart.
Moreover, the definite article indicates that he
was a well-known brother. He is also described
as a *"faithful minister";* in other words, a
trustworthy, steadfast preacher of the Gospel.
He is as well a *"fellow servant in the Lord,"*
the apostle's sympathizing associate, one who
sympathized with him in his views of the Gospel, and doing so *in the Lord,* having with Paul
a blessed experience of the preciousness of the
Gospel. He was sent to Colossæ not merely to
carry the epistle, but also to give to the Christians there all the news about the apostle; to
make known to them its circumstances and his
firmness in the faith. And this would comfort
their hearts, encouraging them in their fight
with error. Onesimus was a runaway slave of
Philemon. He was from "among" the Colossians, and, accordingly, was now being sent
back home. Sent back home, however, as a
"faithful and beloved brother." Sent back to
his master, but no more to be regarded as only
a slave, but now a brother; no longer as dis-
honest, but trustworthy; no longer an object

of contempt, but of love (Phil. ii. 16). He also is designated *"the"* faithful and beloved brother, one who had evidently been marked and observed as such. His being sent back in the company of Tychicus was a measure of prudence towards him, inasmuch as it rendered more certain the Christian reception of the returning slave.

Secondly, let us consider the section covering the greetings from brethren as found in verses 10 to 14:

"Aristarchus, my fellow prisoner, saluteth you, and Mark, the cousin of Barnabas (touching whom ye received commandments; if he come unto you receive him), and Jesus who is called Justus; who are of the circumcision. These only are my fellow-workers unto the Kingdom of God, such as have been a comfort to me. Epaphras, who is from among you, a servant of Christ Jesus saluteth you, always striving earnestly for you in his prayers, that ye may stand fast, perfect and having been fully assured in all the will of God. For I bear him record that he hath much toiled for you, and those in Laodicea, and those in Hierapolis. Luke, the physician, the beloved one, greeteth you and Demas."

Aristarchus, Mark and Jesus Justus are in a group by themselves. For further reference to the first-named, see Acts xix. 29 and xx. 4. Paul speaks of him as a *"fellow prisoner,"* while Epaphras is his "fellow servant," as indicated in chapter i.   But in Philemon xxiii. we find that Epaphras is the "fellow-prisoner" of the apostle, and Aristarchus his "fellow-laborer."   Now as Colossians and Philemon were written on the same occasion, how shall this reversal and interchange of titles be explained?   Perhaps they were each the fellow-prisoner of Paul, only voluntarily and by turns. During the writing of Colossians, Aristarchus may have been imprisoned with him, while during the writing of Philemon this may have been true of Epaphras.   For other references to Mark, see, for example, Acts xii. 12.   He was associated with Paul in his earlier missionary journey (Acts xii. 25), but separated himself and left the work (Acts xiii. 13), which caused a dispute between Paul and Barnabas, Mark's cousin, or uncle, leading to a separation between them (Acts xv. 26-40).   Our text is the first mention of Mark since the occurrence of that separation about twelve years earlier, and is a commendatory notice.   The nature of the commandments here spoken of as having been sent to the Colossians concerning Mark we do not know, but since the apostle bespeaks his reception by them, those commandments may have referred to this favorable change of opinion about him.   Doubtless the Pauline portion of the churches had come to

look on Mark with suspicion, which now the
apostle decides to efface, since Mark had re-
covered his good opinion, thereafter continuing
to preserve it (II. Tim. iv. 11). It would seem
from this reference to Timothy, that Mark subsequently visited Colossæ, being no doubt received there in love and confidence. As to
Jesus Justus, two others in the New Testament
have his surname (Acts i. 23 and xviii. 17),
but since neither of them can be identified with
him, we know nothing further of him. These
three, however, Aristarchus, Mark and Jesus
Justus, were "of the circumcision"; that is, they
were converted to the Gospel from among the
Jews. And they were evidently the only
Jewish co-workers with Paul unto the "Kingdom of God" then with him at Rome. At least,
they were the only ones who had been "a comfort" or encouragement to him. Of course,
this does not mean that there were only three
persons among the Christians at Rome who
were converted Jews, but only that these three
were the only converted Jews who really sympathized with him in his view of the Kingdom
of God (Eph. iii. 2, 6), and so worked with
him as to have been a comfort to him. These
three sent their greetings to the Colossian
church. Epaphras sent his also, but he was
"from among them," himself a Colossian, and

"*a servant of Jesus Christ.*" This last-mentioned title Paul gives only to himself, to Timothy (Phil. i. 1), and to Epaphras. The greetings of Epaphras are significant, for he "*strove earnestly in his prayers*" for Colossians. He wrestled in prayer that they might "*stand fast,*" being "*perfect*"; that is, perfect in the perfection of Christ, an expression already sufficiently explained. While thus perfect in Christ he would have them "*fully assured in all the will of God,*" which means fully assured according to that will, realizing their perfection in Christ and being enabled to stand fast for that reason. The apostle was a witness to the "*toil*" of this brother on their behalf, and not only on their behalf, as he adds, but on behalf of the brethren in Laodicea and Hierapolis. Luke and Demas also sent greetings. The first-named is the author of the third gospel and of the Acts of the Apostles, and was known as "the physician." In Acts xvi. 10 he speaks of himself as attached to Paul. In Galatians iv. 13, 14 the latter speaks of his constitutional malady, whatever it may have been, as having troubled him at a certain time, and since the occasion referred to by him and that spoken of by Luke are synchronous, it is supposed that Luke's' companionship originated at that time. He is not the physician merely, but "*the be-*

loved one," whom Paul thus gratefully names.
Doubtless he was not of Jewish birth like the
earlier mentioned trio. As to Demas, it is significant that his name stands here with no
commendation whatever. In II. Timothy iv,
10, he is mentioned only to be contrasted with
Luke, which suggests the thought that his de-
fection had already begun to foreshadow itself.

The third division, as we have seen, includes
the apostle's salutations to particular friends,
and reads as follows:

"Salute the brethren in Laodicea, and Nymphas
and the church in their house. And when this epistle
is read among you, cause that it be read also in the
church of the Laodiceans; and that ye likewise read
that from Laodicea. And say to Archippus, Take
heed to the ministry, which thou didst receive in the
Lord, that thou fulfil it" (15-17).

"The brethren in Laodicea" seems to desig-
nate a special circle of brethren in that church,
and perhaps of smaller comprehension than
that indicated by the phrase in the next verse,
which speaks of "the church of the Laodiceans." Indeed, the allusion to "Nymphas and
the church in their house" may explain who are
meant by "the brethren in Laodicea." It may
mean Epaphras, and his family and friends
who worshipped in his house. Compare here
Romans xvi. 19, and Philemon ii. for other

references to churches in houses. There is no
clear example of a separate building being devoted to Christian worship in the Roman world
before the third century, apartments in houses
being used for that purpose. The thought of a
church in a house is very beautiful, and just
what it was like we may gather from Acts xii.
12. (See also Matt. xviii. 20.) Paul's special
message to the Colossians as a whole is very
interesting as showing that he desired his epistle to be read to the whole church, and also to
the church of the Laodiceans. Moreover, that
from Laodicea must be read at Colossæ, indicating that an interchange of epistles was perhaps customary even in those early days, and
offering a hint as to the apparatus employed by
the Church of the first centuries in determining
the canon of the New Testament. Here was a
circulation of teachings and a searching into
the Holy Scriptures by all the Christians of
every place. An interesting inquiry concerns
that epistle from Laodicea. To what epistle
does Paul refer? Probably that which we call
the epistle to the Ephesians, for it was sent at
the same time as that to Colossæ, and by the
same messengers. Moreover, it is free from all
local allusions, which would hardly have been
the case had it been addressed to the church in
Ephesus exclusively, where the writer had ex-

ercised his ministry for three years. According to Tischendorf, the name "Ephesus," in the first verse of that epistle, is omitted in both the Sinaitic and Vatican manuscripts. It may, therefore, have been a circular letter addressed to the leading churches of proconsular Asia. If so, Tychicus would be furnished with several copies of it, depositing one at Colossæ, another at Laodicea, and so on. Finally, Paul addresses himself to Archippus, who may have been located as a minister of the Gospel at either of the two cities, Colossæ or Laodicea. He had *received* "the ministry" in the sense that the Lord Jesus had called him into it. But he had received it *"in the Lord,"* as indicating his own personal experience of the preciousness of Christ. And perhaps he had received it from the Lord by the hands of Paul, for the aorist tense he employs points to a definite time and act of reception—"thou *didst* receive." He must *"take heed"* to this ministry to fulfil it, to discharge it in the accuracy and fullness of the teachings of the Gospel. In order to do this he must study the Word, consecrating himself to the work in pains and toil. And why was this message to Archippus not sent directly to him, but to the church at large to be delivered to him? Was it that the church itself might be stirred up to feel its own responsibility in regard to its ministers? If the latter are to watch over the church, then the church is to watch over them also as regards their life and teachings. There is a sense, therefore, in which this message to the individual was a message to the whole church.

Fourth, we now reach the last division of these "Personal Greetings," which is devoted to the apostle's autograph salutations, verse 18:

"The salutation by the hand of me, Paul. Remember my bonds. Grace be with you."

The letter was doubtless dictated to an amanuensis (Rom. xvi. 22), but the closing words were written with his own hand, which seems, indeed, to have been his general practice, for he calls attention to it in some places (I. Cor. xvi. 21; II. Thess. iii. 17). But sometimes his autograph extends to more than the closing sentence, as in Galatians vi. 11, and the following verses, while his letter to Philemon was entirely written by himself (19). He appeals to them to remember his *"bonds,"* but this appeal is not so much for himself as for his teachings, as we gather from Ephesians iii. 1, iv. 1. As the Colossians remembered that in writing his autograph the chain upon his right hand was moving along the paper, the sublime teachings it contained would come to them with added emphasis as to their truth and preciousness. His closing words are the same as those in other of his epistles. In speaking of grace he uses the definite article, "*The* grace be with you," as though the expression had by this time established its own meaning as indicating the unsearchable riches of Christ, and no longer required the addition of His name as in the case of his earlier epistles.

33

THE SUMMING UP

WE have now completed our exposition of this great epistle, and from the opening address to the closing salutation, we have followed the apostle step by step, examining and weighing his words as we have been able. What an immense extent of truth have we passed over, and with how many of the fundamental and most precious doctrines of the Gospel have we been brought in contact! Many of the truths considered were in the nature of crucial tests of the opinions and speculations of men of the first Christian century, and equally so of the philosophers of our own century. In closing our meditations, therefore, let us give a rapid and general review of the leading lessons we have been taught:—

First. We have seen that the practical end in view of Christianity is holy living and personal blessedness. You will recall how the soul's union and communion with God is presented and urged throughout the whole epistle as the prime and fundamental need of our nature. Our holy living is never possible apart from God. He is the object of the soul's worship, and the principle of the soul's true culture. His authority is sacred and supreme, hence when we are separated from Him we are in a state of sin and moral disability. The very ground swell of the entire epistle shows us that there is no holy living except as in union with God. Now add to this teaching those exhortations of the third chapter, where we are vigorously urged to put off the old man and put on the new in the various relations of life, and consider how that these exhortations are the focus in which have converged all the doctrinal teachings of the preceding portion of the epistle. All this is holy living. In it is involved the Christian's personal blessedness, for it is the soul's true culture. It shows us the Christian with peace really in his heart, joy singing from his lips, and hope apprehending and triumphing in the very title of Eternal Glory. This is the practical end in view of the Christian religion.

Second. Our epistle has shown us also, that before we can come into this condition of union and communion with God, we must have had redemption, forgiveness of sins, reconciliation with God and the new birth. These are the essential prerequisites in the case. Now in God's plan, forgiveness presupposes redemp-

tion already effected, for He will not permit
His forgiveness to operate in such a way as to
become a premium for committing sin. He
will not treat sin lightly, nor look upon it with
the least allowance. He will maintain His law,
hence the teaching we find in chapter I., verse
14 and 20-22. Apart from the redemption
which is in Christ there can be no holy living.
No resolutions, or reformations or religious
services can avail to produce it. The condemnation must be taken away, and Christ's finished work for us does alone accomplish that.
Then, too, as sinners we are not only guilty
of certain acts of transgression, but are full of
sins, "dead in sins," without life. We need,
then, the gift of life to rise out of our natural
death and be placed in possession of the new
man. Otherwise we cannot think, or feel or
act in accordance with the fact of our redemption in Christ. We cannot, because we will
not. We must first be quickened out of our
death and brought into a simple reception of
the Lord Jesus Christ.

Third. Accordingly, our epistle elaborately
presents the only and sufficient mediatorship
of Christ (i. 21, 22). So perfect is his mediatorship that we and He are one (2, 11-13, 3,
1.) Thus "we are complete in Him," or rather
"we are in Him, having been filled full." No

traditions of men, no false philosophy, no religious ritual must be allowed for a single instant to take His place in our thoughts and confidence, or to dim the glory of His all-sufficiency.

Fourth. As mediator, He is also God, and neither angel, nor emanation nor creature. He is God Incarnate (1:15-17). Not only may we rest on His mediatorial work as perfect, but in every contact of our hearts with Him we are brought in contact direct with God.

Fifth. Accordingly, in Him God the Father is put into active connection with us. A thought which is one of the leading revelations of the epistle. The Gnostic heresy, relegated God to an infinite distance from any personal intercourse with sinful man, and that old Gnosticism, though in many a modified form still prevails. It is thought by many that He is too great to concern Himself with our individual needs, or that He is too much the God of law and order to interpose for our relief from consequences of sin; or for different reasons He is not thought to love us or care for us or, personally, to come into intercourse with us. Indeed, the whole of this false philosophy is shivered into fragments by the authoritative pronouncement of this epistle. The Almighty and Eternal God *is* concerned about us, *does* love us, *does* interpose for our salvation, *does* hold communion with us. Not only is a believer in Christ saved, but he is privileged to joy in God. Jesus Christ is the Father's way to us and our way to the Father, and blessed indeed is the meeting. We are sinners, but in Christ our sins are put away, and whoever refuses to come to the Father on account of his unworthiness, has simply alleged his unworthiness in a spirit of self-righteousness, and is unwilling to appear before the Father in the worthiness of his sponsor and Saviour, God Incarnate.

Sixth. From all this it results that the power of holy living is the heart's realization of the mediation of Christ. The way of access to God has been provided, the redemption is perfectly accomplished, the believer's union with his Saviour in death and resurrection is a wondrous fact; the new birth, pardon and acceptance, heirship of the kingdom of the Heavens, and thus the possibility of the holy living, all these are established facts. If then, all this is clearly understood, appreciated appropriated and rejoiced in, shall not the believer run in the way of God's commandments? Shall there not be a power within springing into the presence of God with the gladness of a child? Does not the realization of Christ's

relationship to the believer demonstrate to him
how wondrously God loves him? And does
not that kindle his own love to God? And what
is so strong as love, or so laborious, or so pa-
tient, or so joyous, or so enduring? Yes, this
is the power of a holy life.

Seventh. Hence the necessity of being on
our guard against enticing words of men. If
the above-mentioned truth is all-important to
holy living, then must we keep our conceptions
clear. But enticing words of men are sounding
all around us. The air is full of false reasonings in persuasive discourse. We are evermore
in danger of beguilement, and of having our
thoughts about Christ confused and enfeebled.
For this reason it is that the Word of Christ
must be permitted to dwell in us in all wisdom.

Eighth. Finally we derive from our epistle
the assurance of the ultimate triumph of the
Gospel among mankind. This Gospel is the
very truth of God, and He means that it shall
ultimately be universally received. This is
clear inferentially, and is also definitely asserted in Isaiah 11:9. We should not, therefore, be disheartened at the prevalence around
us of Theological falsehoods and of daring ungodliness of life. We should stand fast in our
own testimony to the truth amid the heresies
of professing Christians and the godless rea-

sonings of so-called philosophers. Let us know
the truth serenely, feel it joyously, and promote it actively, for "we serve the Lord
Christ," and

*"BEHOLD, HE COMETH WITH
CLOUDS; AND EVERY EYE SHALL
SEE HIM, AND THOSE WHO PIERCED
HIM; AND ALL THE TRIBES OF THE
LAND SHALL WAIT AT HIM. EVEN
SO. AMEN"* (Rev. i. 7).